Pepter

tomato

leek

Artichoke

Fennel

Chili

Cabbage

Beet

Champignon

Radish

Onion

Asparagus

Carrot

Broccoli

Potato

Avocado

Corn

Garlic

Ginger

Pumpkin

Pepper

Cucumber

tomato

Eggplant

leek

Artichoke

Fennel

Chili

Cabbage

Champignon

Beet

Radish

Onion

Asparagus

Carrot

Potato

Avocado

Broccoli

Corn

Garlic

Ginger

Pumpkin

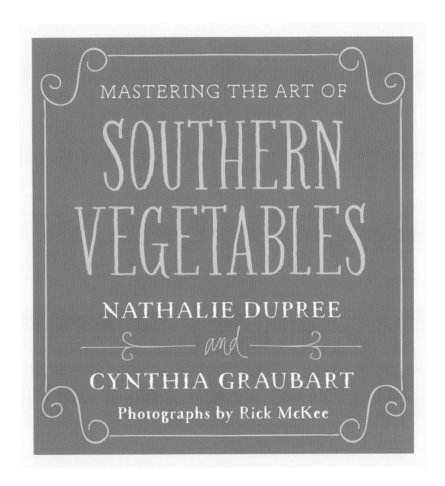

MASTERING THE ART OF

SOUTHERN
VEGETABLES

NATHALIE DUPREE

and

CYNTHIA GRAUBART

Photographs by Rick McKee

GIBBS SMITH
TO ENRICH AND INSPIRE HUMANKIND

To all the wonderful women and some men who have helped me with my books and teaching. —Nathalie Dupree

To Phylecia, my sister and best friend. And the only one who knows my history with peas. —Cynthia Graubart

19 18 17 16 15   5 4 3 2 1

Text © 2015 Nathalie Dupree and Cynthia Graubart
Photographs © 2015 Rick McKee

Published by
Gibbs Smith
P.O. Box 667
Layton, Utah 84041

1.800.835.4993 orders
www.gibbs-smith.com

Designed by Rita Sowins
Printed and bound in Hong Kong

Gibbs Smith books are printed on paper produced from sustainable PEFC-certified forest/controlled wood source. Learn more at www.pefc.org.

Library of Congress Cataloging-in-Publication Data

Dupree, Nathalie.
  Mastering the art of Southern vegetables / Nathalie Dupree and Cynthia Graubart ; photographs by Rick McKee. — First edition.
     pages cm
  Includes index.
  ISBN 978-1-4236-3738-7
1. Cooking, Vegetables. 2. Cooking, American—Southern style.
I. Graubart, Cynthia Stevens. II. Title.
  TX801.D88 2015
  641.6'5—dc23
                          2014024267

ACKNOWLEDGMENTS

To the many that labor in the background, testing recipes, proof reading, helping to tote equipment, assisting with food photography and more, thank you again, Elizabeth (Bea) Shaffer, Lisa Moore, Nicole Marriner, Sarah Gaedes, Patty Scott, Pat Royalty, Francine Wolfe Schwartz, Alice Levkoff, and all the many others who helped with this and other facets of our culinary lives.

Our team of testers under the supreme direction of Beth Price provided valuable feedback, and we are so appreciative of their contributions: Currie Donna Currie, Tina Eib, Melody Elliott-Koontz, Mary Grande, Crystal Joyce, Karen Depp, Annmarie Kostyk, Marlene Lockett, Catherine Daum Lucas, Diane Miller, Maria Purwin, Debra Rogers, Pat Royalty, Dawn Stribling, Kim Underwood, and Francine Wolfe Schwartz.

We also thank our talented kitchen director/ food stylist, Mallory DeGolian.

CONTENTS

FOREWORD

Once upon a time, not so long ago, there were three little words guaranteed to strike fear and loathing into the hearts of our children:

"Eat your vegetables."

Perhaps with good reason. Those were the days when string beans were often stewed with fatback until they were wrinkled and shriveled, cooked carrots could be smeared on the plate like orange paste, and green peas often resembled furry green BBs.

But that time is no more. Now vegetables star in the toniest restaurants, adorn chic dinner plates from Malibu to East Hampton, and have tastes to make the angels sing.

In this book, my friends Cynthia Graubart and Nathalie Dupree have gathered 120 vegetable recipes that will make you a star and your guests happier than pigs in—well, you know.

As for those long-ago children, happily, they grew up.

So did vegetables.

—Anne Rivers Siddons

INTRODUCTION

While filming more than 100 television episodes, we traveled all over the South and enjoyed seeing how and where its vegetables are grown. We ate tomatoes from the hills of western North Carolina and ripe melons from the sandy fields of southern Georgia. The Georgia Commissioner of Agriculture loaned us his plane, and we loaded its storage area with zucchini, squash and Vidalia onions to take home. We watched as onions were pulled from the ground, laid out to dry, stored and shipped. We visited fields with sivvy beans as far as the eye could see, and we pulled up Jerusalem artichokes, their sunflower seeds scattering to the winds. We dug sweet potatoes and tiny white potatoes, pulled up peanuts, and watched as cucumbers were pickled. We realized then, as we do now, what a boon it was to be in a region with two to three growing seasons and a cuisine as wide and deep as the region itself.

Our region spans the East Coast from Maryland to Florida and westward across to Texas, encompassing a range of ethnicities as well as a variety of climates and soils, all of which create a diverse and rich selection of vegetables to choose from. Many cultures and many peoples have contributed to the lexicon of Southern cooking, primarily those from Africa, England, Spain, and France.

The South's economy has had many ups and downs that impacted the food. Regardless, fresh vegetables have long been the stars of the Southern plate. For the average agrarian family, home gardens, little plots that fed a family almost all year long, enabled them to avoid spending cash money for food and save it for other necessities. Meat—primarily pork—which was particularly important as a source of energy for those who worked in the fields all day, was relegated to important meals, such as Sunday dinner or a holiday, or added as an important protein and flavor enhancer to vegetables.

Although the South has a long agricultural history, the expanding farm-to-table movement has again increased knowledge of the growing number of vegetables available to the home cook. More of us are growing our own vegetables or seeking out those grown locally or regionally, with less travel and storage time en route. Farmers are indulging their creative streaks and developing multicolored beets, bell peppers, tomatoes, and other vegetables. There are more vegetable options than ever before, and these are exciting as well as tasty, filling, and nutritious, bringing dashes of color, enticing aromas, and variety to our tables.

In addition to the impressive new varieties of vegetables being grown, seed banks and agricultural historians are reviving heirloom varieties of vegetables that languished in years past in favor of vegetables that shipped better, were uniform in size, and were, quite frankly, tasteless. The packs that contained three pale tomatoes are nearly banished, with tomatoes of deep color and rich, earthy taste winning out, enticing us all to eat more and better.

Chefs make a vital contribution to Southern vegetables, shaving and ribboning them, roasting, grilling, broiling, boiling, and braising them in new ways with new varieties and new sauces. They have shown us it possible to use just a small amount of one ingredient mixed with small amounts of others to make a whole dish, in a way that accommodates a garden's irregular production. Continual improvement

in freezing and preserving methods maximize both freshness and the number of months during a year that vegetables grace our Southern tables.

With the ever-growing variety of vegetables and ways to cook them, it is no wonder that the largest, and coincidentally our favorite, chapter in our book *Mastering the Art of Southern Cooking* is "Vegetables and Sides." Here we present our favorite vegetable recipes from that book alongside many new ones. We have tried to enhance the flavors for which Southern cooking is known with the new techniques and ingredients while also retaining the traditional. We have honored as well as varied old favorites such as creamed corn. For instance, corn itself has experienced a change-up, with even the corncob now being used as a stock to increase tastiness and nutrition—something unheard of in even the thriftiest of household in my youth.

These recipes use ingredients readily available and often grown in the South, with a few upscale ingredients from "away" (like Parmigiano-Reggiano cheese) that enhance just about any vegetable and have been imported to the this region since the days of Thomas Jefferson. Spices have long been available in the South, arriving in our ports in Galveston, New Orleans, Savannah, and

Charleston, among others. Some of the imports, most famously coconut, are used in dishes that are typically considered Southern even though they are not grown here. We have added the meat flavorings—fat back, bacon, ham, etc.—that are part of traditional Southern cooking, but certainly they, too, can be omitted and other flavorings added.

Many side dishes—those served on the side of meat for a large meal such as Sunday dinner—are included in this book. For reasons of space, we have not included rice- or pasta-based dishes even though there are a number of these in Mastering the Art of Southern Cooking. We hope you will turn there if you feel the lack. In general, we don't mean for any of these vegetable dishes to stand alone as a meal. They will serve well under a roast chicken or alongside a pot roast. Or, of course, as a time-honored vegetable plate.

We have kept the home cook in mind, as we do for all our books. These recipes are, for the most part, unexacting. After all, vegetables don't follow a recipe themselves—they come out willy-nilly at their own speed and in their own way and size. They grow according to the whim of the season and the climate. So with this book comes permission and encouragement to swap out, add, subtract, and change the recipes to suit what is available. We share what we have learned so that you will have confidence in serving a variety of vegetable dishes in ways that become your favorites or that you might not have known before. We hope you will enjoy being creative in your kitchen as much as we do in ours.

GENERAL VEGETABLE INFORMATION

COOKING VEGETABLES

Stovetop cooking vegetables—To blanch, add tender green or small vegetables to boiling water for just 3 to 4 minutes, depending on size, until crisp-tender. Run under cold water and drain. Add whole root vegetables to cold water, bring to the boil, and cook for 15 to 20 minutes, depending on size and density, until nearly cooked. Drain quickly, reserve the liquid for soups if desired, and run vegetables under cold water to stop the cooking.

Roasting vegetables—Oven-roasting vegetables allows the natural sugars to caramelize, giving a whole new taste dimension to most any vegetable. Line a rimmed baking sheet with foil, toss 1 to 1^1/$_2$ pounds of the cut vegetable in oil, and spread out in an even layer on a baking sheet. Halfway through the roasting time, toss or turn the vegetables for even cooking. See chart on roasting vegetables for further guidelines, page 199.

Microwaving vegetables—Fresh vegetables are appealing when prepared in the microwave, and some studies suggest the vegetables retain more of their nutrients when cooked this way. Utilizing uniform pieces and a microwave-safe container, add 1 tablespoon of water for each ^{1}/$_2$ pound of vegetables. Cover with microwave-safe plastic wrap or a glass lid. For ^{1}/$_2$ pound of vegetables, cook on high for 4 minutes. Check the tenderness of the vegetables with a fork, and continue to check in 30-second increments until the vegetable reaches desired tenderness. Tender vegetables will need only 4 or 5 minutes. Tougher, thicker vegetables will need longer.

Refreshing green vegetables—Running green vegetables under cold water stops the cooking and sets the color, causing them to look "refreshed." Chefs specify ice water, but I find ice isn't necessary with small home quantities of vegetables.

Reheating vegetables—All vegetables may be made ahead and reheated. When reheating boiled or steamed vegetables, there are several methods that may be used:

- Heat fat, such as oil, butter, duck fat, etc., in a frying pan, add the vegetables, and quickly heat, stirring rapidly. (Or use a non-stick pan with no fat added.)

- Arrange the vegetables in one layer in an ovenproof pan, cover with foil, and leave in a 350-degree preheated oven until heated through. Start with 5 minutes for small, thin vegetables, or heat up to 15 to 20 minutes for thick ones, learning to know oven and pan, until confident the timing is correct.

- Return the vegetables to boiling liquid briefly to heat through.

- Warm in a microwave oven.

- Steam, grill or broil, or sauté.

USING EXTRA PRODUCE

I'm haunted by the dribs and drabs of food in my refrigerator, and I blame the farmers market for the lush tomatoes and vivid red and yellow bell peppers that I overbuy to keep on the table—ignoring them until they are on the edge of extinction. Eggplants, with their thick skins, always seem so sturdy and indestructible that I ignore their girth when I purchase them, only to be frustrated when they take up the whole refrigerator vegetable bin. And who ever purchased one ear of corn? (Even though corn is a refrigerator hog with its husks on, it is

so much better that way it is worth it. There's always one that will not fit on the grill and languishes lonely and forgotten until desperation meets dinnertime. Fortunately, restaurants have set the stage by serving scattered bits of vegetables. So what if there isn't enough of one thing to feed everyone what would be considered a portion? A few dribs and drabs of everything will make an empty plate look like a vegetable repast. Or stretch it—let them eat a bit of Maque Choux (page 83), which happily accommodates shrimp, or Southern Ratatouille (page 93) tucked underneath a cooked chicken breast.

GLOBE ARTICHOKES

Artichokes are flower buds picked before they mature. A member of the thistle family, they have tough, thorny leaves that grow out of a fleshy, succulent base known as the bottom or, incorrectly, the heart. The bottom is covered with an edible, but undesirable, hairy choke that should be removed.

Baby artichokes are not babies at all, but fully mature artichokes that are smaller because they grew close to the ground and were sheltered by larger leaves on the plant. They have a tender choke and are, therefore, entirely edible and easier to prepare. These are often found in jars, canned, or frozen, and are also incorrectly called artichoke hearts.

Select artichokes with tightly packed leaves that are not discolored. Larger, older artichokes are tougher but make a prettier presentation. The longer an artichoke has been on the grocer's shelf, the more dehydrated it will be. Refresh it by trimming off the stem and covering the artichoke with ice-cold water for 30 minutes, or refrigerate in water for up to 2 days.

TRIMMING AND PREPARING ARTICHOKES

To trim and prepare an artichoke for cooking, wash with cold water and cut the stem off, leaving a level base, so that the artichoke will rest on its base. Save the stem, as it is a flavorful extension of the artichoke heart and edible when peeled. It makes a good snack dipped in butter after being steamed or boiled.

Peel the tough outer leaves, snapping at the interior pale green, and discard. Cut off the top fourth of the artichoke (about an inch) with kitchen scissors, or lay it on its side and cut down across the top with a large sharp knife. Trim off the thorny tips of the remaining leaves with scissors. Artichokes will turn brown when cut. Rub the cut parts of the artichoke with a sliced lemon to prevent browning.

Basic Globe Artichokes

SERVES 4

This is the most common method of cooking artichokes, tenderizing the leaves and making them pliable and easier to remove, as well as cooking the bottom. There are many edible parts of globe artichokes—the little tender crescent of pale green that attaches each leaf to the main frame, the center portion (called the bottom) after the thistle (choke) part is scraped off, and the peeled stem. The bottoms may be prepared as below and served cut into quarters or served whole as a "plate" for salad.

4 artichokes, trimmed

1 cup butter or mayonnaise

Hot sauce, optional

Trim the artichokes and add them to a pot of boiling salted water. To keep them from bobbing up, spread a tea towel over the artichokes in the water and cover with a pie plate or other heatproof plate. Reduce heat, cover with a lid, and cook 30 to 45 minutes, until a leaf pulls out easily. Uncover the pot and carefully remove the lid or plate and tea towel before removing artichokes and draining them on a plate.

Serve at room temperature with melted butter or cold with mayonnaise. Add a few drops of hot sauce to the butter or mayonnaise if desired.

Cool slightly and eat by pulling off the leaves, dipping the pale green bottom portion of the leaf into the butter or mayonnaise, and scraping just that portion with the teeth for a tender morsel. Proceed around the artichoke until all the leaves are gone, eating just the tender portions. In the center is the artichoke bottom, shaped like a small bowl. If there is any remaining choke (a furry coating inside), spoon out and discard it. To enjoy this prime piece of artichoke, cut the bowl into bite-sized pieces and dip in the sauce. The detached stem may be peeled and eaten this way as well.

Variation: Steamed Artichokes

Tie the artichokes together with string so they don't bobble around. Move to a rack in a large pot with a small amount of water inside. Cover and cook until tender, as above, monitoring the water level and adding more if in danger of boiling dry.

Variation: Microwaved Artichokes

Add trimmed artichokes to a glass dish with water to a depth of less than $1/2$ inch. Cover tightly and microwave on high power for 7 minutes for 1 artichoke and up to 15 to 20 minutes for 4, checking every 4 or so minutes for tenderness.

Stuffed Artichokes

Stuffed Artichokes

SERVES 4

New Orleans restaurants serve stuffed artichokes, based on the strong Italian influence on the cuisine in that region. The "stuffing" goes between the leaves and makes a splashy presentation. As with most restaurant preparations, it takes a bit more time than home-cooked dishes.

1 cup breadcrumbs, or panko

1 cup freshly grated Parmesan cheese

3 green onions, or scallions, chopped

2 teaspoons capers

4 garlic cloves, finely chopped

Finely chopped fresh parsley

Salt

Freshly ground black pepper

4 trimmed globe artichokes (page 14)

½ cup oil

Stir together the breadcrumbs, cheese, green onions, capers, and garlic, adding parsley, and salt and pepper to taste, or process in a food processor. Turn each trimmed artichoke upside down and press lightly against the counter to open the leaves. In the center of the artichoke is the choke, an inedible thistly barrier to the succulent artichoke bottom. Turn the artichoke right side up and remove the choke with a spoon, leaving the bottom intact. Fill the spaces among the leaves with the bread stuffing, using a small spoon to wedge open the space and insert the stuffing. Put any remaining stuffing into the hollow left by removing the choke. Brush the artichokes liberally with oil.

Move the artichokes to a rack in a big pot with a little water under the rack. Cover and steam for 45 minutes, or until a leaf pulls off easily. Check occasionally, being careful of steam, to be sure there is still water in the pot. Or microwave, covered with plastic wrap, on high power for 10 minutes. This may be done up to a day in advance. When ready to serve, run under the broiler until the stuffing is crisped and brown and the artichokes are heated through.

GREEN ONIONS

Green onions are the early, immature onion, with a sharper, brighter flavor. The greens can be substituted for scallion greens. Vidalia green onions are larger than the average medium onion and are frequently roasted whole in season. The term "green onion" is used interchangeably by many of us for "scallions," their baby cousin.

JERUSALEM "SUNCHOKE" ARTICHOKES

These tasty knobby roots are neither from Jerusalem nor are they artichokes. They were so named because they taste very similar to globe artichokes. In fact, they are a type of sunflower, also known as sunchokes. They have an outer skin much like a potato, so scrub them well. They can be peeled or cooked in their skin and are delicious sautéed, baked, grilled, broiled, roasted, or boiled. Raw, they are crisp and refreshing in a salad.

Sautéed Jerusalem Artichokes

SERVES 4

I grew Jerusalem artichokes in the garden of our restaurant near Social Circle, Georgia. First I enjoyed looking at the sunflowers, and then I had the artichokes. They were a constant on our menu all summer—sautéed, roasted, grilled, or broiled, cooked the same way as a small potato.

1 pound Jerusalem artichokes, halved or quartered if large

Butter or oil

Salt or sea salt

Freshly ground black pepper

Heat a skillet over medium heat and melt butter to coat the bottom of the pan. Add the scrubbed chokes and sauté until tender, about 12 to 18 minutes, turning frequently. Season to taste with salt and pepper.

Variation: Boiled Jerusalem Artichokes

Bring the scrubbed or peeled artichokes to the boil in enough salted water to cover. Boil until fork tender, about 10 to 15 minutes. Drain. Peel, if necessary, and cut into pieces as desired according to size, or eat small ones whole. Season to taste with butter, salt, and pepper.

Sautéed Jerusalem Artichokes

ASPARAGUS

When the first asparagus pokes its head up in the Lowcountry, we know it is spring. The newer varieties in the early twenty-first century include slender purple or green stalks as long as a forearm and as thin as a pencil. They are so sweet they can pleasurably be eaten raw, although rarely are.

One amazing thing about asparagus is how many personalities it has. Whether crisply cool, subtly room temperature, or hot and dripping with butter or sauce, it adds grace and refinement to a meal. While asparagus comes in many sizes, We prefer the thin, finger-size ones. If using the thin ones, allow more stalks per person. They cook quickly and are often eaten with the fingers. Larger asparagus need peeling and are best cooked standing up in a tall poacher—much like an old-time metal coffee pot—the theory being that the stems cook in the water while the tips steam.

When purchasing asparagus ahead of time, keep the stem ends moist by standing upright in about a half-inch of water in the refrigerator or lying on the refrigerator shelf in a plastic bag with the ends wrapped in wet paper towels.

Cooked asparagus can be refrigerated and served cold at a later time, or quickly heated in a microwave or under a broiler and served as a hot vegetable to accompany a meal. If not using the cooked asparagus within a few days, freeze in plastic ziplock bags. Thaw and reheat when needed. Tightly wrapped, cooked asparagus can be kept frozen for up to 3 months. It will lose its crunch but will be fine for soup or a casserole.

EATING ASPARAGUS

Traditionally, and according to Emily Post, asparagus is a finger food. Cooked properly rather than overcooked, it is still crisp and difficult to cut, shooting across the table if attempted. Cook only until its stem has the slightest bend—a decided droop is far too much. Sauced asparagus is handled with individual asparagus tongs, or hot damp cloths are passed to clean any messy fingers after eating.

ASPARAGUS IN
SOUTHERN HISTORY

Asparagus is a fascinating vegetable to grow. Some varieties take up to 7 years to poke their first wispy shoots up above the ground. Once up, however, they grow rapidly, and the gardener fears going away for a few days lest they have grown and gone. South Carolina was at one time a major grower and supplier of asparagus.

In a 1745 issue of *London Magazine*, the author writes that along the Georgia coast, "the good Indians regaled us and for Greens, boiled us the Tops of China-Briars, which eat almost as well as Asparagus." In *Charleston Receipts*, the recipe for "Chainey Briar" calls for 2 bunches of chainey briar (wild asparagus), cooking them as one would fresh asparagus. The top of a wild bush, chainey briars were considered an early substitute for asparagus.

"Sparrow Grass" was asparagus in the eighteenth century in both England and America. "Sprue," the first thinning of the growing asparagus, is the long-awaited sign of spring.

Basic Asparagus

SERVES 4

It would take a very tall asparagus poacher to cook the thin asparagus—hardly suitable anyway, as they cook quickly and the stem is cooked just about the time the tip is—so I use a deep frying pan.

1 pound asparagus	Salt
2–4 tablespoons butter or oil	Freshly ground black pepper

Fill a deep frying pan or chicken fryer (non-iron to avoid discoloration), large enough to hold the asparagus lying down, three-quarters full of salted water. Bring to the boil with the salt. Add the asparagus to the pan, all facing the same way, in batches if necessary, with the stems in the water and the tips hanging just over the edge of the pan. Cook 3 to 5 minutes, depending on the size of the asparagus and the color. The asparagus are cooked when they are crisp-tender and bend ever so slightly but are still bright green. Remove from the pot, drain, and rinse in cold water to set the color and stop the cooking. Drain again and set aside. The asparagus can be held at room temperature for a few hours or covered with plastic wrap and refrigerated for serving later. They are good hot or cold or at room temperature.

If serving cold, toss in olive oil, salt, and pepper, then cover and refrigerate.

If reheating cooked asparagus to serve hot, heat the frying pan with the butter or oil, add the asparagus, and toss quickly over the heat until heated through. (Use fingers or a pair of tongs to keep them moving so all are heated but none are overcooked). Turn out onto a platter and serve. They will turn an ugly gray if doused with citrus juice or vinegar, so use one or several of the following variations on page 24 for flavor.

Basic Asparagus

Roasted and Grilled Asparagus

SERVES 4

These are two delicious methods of cooking asparagus, but they are very dependent on the thickness of the asparagus, so take care.

1 pound asparagus	Salt
2–4 tablespoons oil	Freshly ground black pepper

Preheat oven or grill to 450 degrees or preheat broiler. Toss asparagus with oil, and spread them into a single layer on a rimmed baking sheet, oven rack, or grill. Bake in the oven, broil two inches from broiler, or cook on the grill. They are best if browned slightly, but cook to your preference.

Variations:

- Serve with melted butter.
- Toss with grated orange and/or lemon rind for a citrus flavor. Or toss with grated ginger, buttered crumbs, herbs, roasted pecans, walnuts, or pine nuts.
- Add to salads and serve cold.
- Toss with cooked mushrooms to reheat.
- Top with $1/2$ pound cooked and peeled shrimp, melted butter, or olive oil.
- Top with slivered ham.

Ribboned (Shaved) Asparagus

SERVES 4

Fresh, tender asparagus are an exceptional spring delight when shaved into thin ribbons and eaten raw. But they are also lovely tossed briefly over heat to just barely warm them.

1 pound asparagus

2–4 tablespoons butter or oil

Salt

Freshly ground black pepper

Grated Parmesan cheese, optional

Cut off any tough ends from the asparagus. Using a vegetable peeler, peel the asparagus from underneath the lowest flower all the way to the cut end. Rotate around the asparagus, continuing until all the asparagus is ribboned. (If you are left with a small interior portion, put it on the counter and cut thinly.)

To eat cold, drizzle with oil, and season with salt and pepper and some Parmesan, or use the asparagus as a bed under a cooked chicken breast or piece of fish.

To eat hot, heat butter or oil in a large pan, add the asparagus ribbons, and toss over heat until just heated through. Season with salt and pepper. Top with Parmesan cheese, if desired.

PEELING ASPARAGUS

The very tiniest spears do not need to be peeled. Tough ends should be cut off, perhaps used for soup at a later time. Snapping is inexact and removes too much of the good part of the asparagus, so that preparation method should be avoided. If the asparagus are fibrous, peel from the stem to the first little flower of the tip. If the asparagus are slender and willowy, it is not necessary to peel them, as that would cause them to bend like weeping willows.

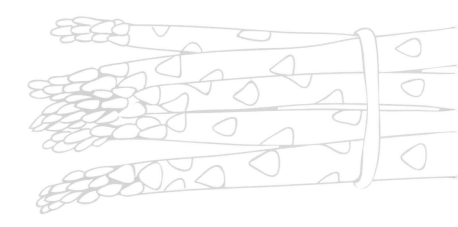

BEANS AND PEAS

Legumes—including peas, beans, peanuts, and lentils—some of the oldest sources of nutrition known to man, have been equally valuable to Southerners throughout the generations and have become one of the South's most beloved vegetables. Long a mainstay of indigent cultures, beans and peas early ensconced themselves in the South, with Thomas Jefferson and others avidly pursuing different types—importing more than 30 varieties himself for experimentation. After the Civil War, beans became as crucial a protein to both black and white families as they were to the earliest settlers.

In a sense, all peas can be beans and all beans can be peas, but we think of peas as something inside the pod and beans the exterior package holding the pea. Actually, many so-called Southern beans are really peas, but are called beans, such as butter beans and their cousin lima beans.

Both peas and beans can be green or dried, and can be "field" or "garden," with dried beans and peas sometimes considered a poor man's necessity available to field hands. Garden peas (called English peas in the South and green peas elsewhere) were considered a richer man's food, perhaps because they are rarely preserved.

GREEN BEANS

The green beans referred to in Southern nomenclature are pole green beans, bunch beans, and half runners. Pole beans, or flat beans, are 6 to 8 inches long and $3/4$ inch wide; they require diligent stringing and are tougher than other green beans. Traditionally cooked long and slow, they are frequently "put up" (canned in jars) for the winter months because they take so well to slow cooking. Bunch beans are the typical green beans found in the grocery store. Half runners are about 4 inches long and $1/3$ inch wide, about the size of a lady's finger, and require only light stringing. The peas inside a half runner pod are barely present; in pole beans, they are more prominent, nearly half the size of lady peas.

Preparing green beans—My mother called cutting or snapping both ends of green beans "tipping and tailing." I prefer cutting to snapping, which removes too much of the bean. Line up the beans next to each other, tough tails together. Cut off the tails. Leave the tips on if desired, or slide the beans so the tips are easily cut off as well.

BLACK-EYED PEAS

These found their way in the early pre-Christian era (1800 bce) to Greece and India, overlapping the "cowpeas." In fifteenth-century Venice, fagioli were originally a black-eyed pea cooked with pork belly or fatback, a precursor to African and Southern methods of seasoning and extracting nutrition and fats for stamina. To confuse the matter, black-eyed peas in the South may be called cowpeas or field peas, and they are the best known of the Southern field peas. They also last longer dried than other peas, which has contributed to their popularity.

Black-eyed peas, rice, and okra were brought to the New World—the Americas and the Caribbean—to feed the slaves, either en route on their horrible journey or while they were here.

As noted in Ken Abala's incredibly informative work *Beans—A History,* corn, beans, and squash (the "three sisters") were essential to the diet of early North Americans, from Aztecs to Virginians, and were described in books as varied as those by Giovanni da Verrazzano in the early 1500s to William Strachey's description in 1612 that the peas the Virginia natives ate were little, like French beans, and the same as *fagioli.* Samuel de Champlain wrote in 1613 of observing "the bean plants twine around the aforementioned corn, which grow to a height of five to six feet." This added nitrogen to the corn.

PEANUTS

A rather sneaky legume, in that the plant grows under the ground and is thought of as a nut (formerly called groundnuts), peanuts are a mainstay of comfort and nutrition in the South. Their arrival from Africa prompted experimentation and development, from boiling and frying them in the shell, to processing them into oils and butters, to just roasting and eating them.

COOKING DRIED LEGUMES

Dried peas and beans expand slowly when cooking, as the only way liquid has to enter is through the little hole called the helium, where the stem was attached. The addition of ingredients early on, such as ham hock, onion, and hot pepper, adds to the flavor from the beginning. The hole expands with the swelling of the beans, so the initial slow penetration speeds up considerably by the end, when the bean has begun to swell up from the liquid between the layers of starch.

A cooked bean can't absorb flavor. At some point, the starch granules burst and "gelatinize," improving the bean's flavor. It is this optimum point the cook strives for—when the bean has its maximum flavor but has not burst like a balloon, losing its flavor to the broth.

To prepare for cooking, pick through the dried beans, removing all stones, and rinse the beans. The rough ratio of dried beans to water is 1 pound of dried beans to approximately 2 cups of water. The processes of soaking dried legumes are varied. Here are several:

1. The standard wisdom of soaking them overnight in a quantity of water to cover is preferable to other methods, as it helps maintain their shape and soften their skins. Drain and discard the water. Overnight soaking decreases the cooking time by 30 minutes, although it is hard for some to remember to start this process the night before.
2. The second most-discussed method is to "quick-soak" them: bring a pot of water to the boil, add the dried legumes, cover the pot with a lid, and let sit 1 hour off the heat. Drain and proceed to cook. This is a bit of a hassle, but it gives a little more bite to the beans, as the skins do not mush as much as in the previous method.
3. The third way is to cook the beans with no prior soaking, which takes one or two hours longer.
4. My solution is to pour boiling water over the dried peas or beans when starting to gather ingredients, drain and discard the water, and proceed with the recipe.

None of these are proven to be superior to others or to have been tested scientifically to determine if the assumptions are sound. What is proven is that long, slow cooking will produce a dried bean that holds its shape and is tender and palatable. Be careful not to stir, or a mush will result.

The longer dried products are on the shelf, the longer they will take to cook. Buy them from a purveyor with frequent turnover.

PREVENTING BOIL OVERS

Peas have a tendency to foam up while cooking and run over the top of the pot. Two ways to prevent this type of boil over are to use a larger pot and/or add a few drops of cooking oil or butter to the water—even a teaspoon will do. Any foam should be removed as it develops.

FREEZING PEAS AND BEANS

Fresh peas freeze very well. When purchasing fresh peas, try to purchase them already snapped—i.e., removed from the pod. Usually there will be some pods that are too small to be opened and have the peas removed. We call those "snaps" and like to have some of them in every package of frozen peas, as they add the flavor of the pod and cook simultaneously. The peas in our market are sold already snapped and in plastic bags. I freeze them as is. When freezing a bulk quantity of peas, spread out on a rimmed baking sheet and move to the freezer; when frozen, pour into plastic ziplock bags and return to the freezer. Since the peas are individually frozen, they will be easy to measure. Cooked beans freeze exceptionally well and are frequently canned or jarred.

SALTING DRIED BEANS AND PEAS

Scientists say salt toughens peas, so if dried beans or peas have not been soaked, err on the side of caution and omit salt until later in the recipe. If they have been soaked, salt the water at the beginning of cooking.

The cooking time of everything depends on size and freshness. Smaller things cook quicker than larger. No one can say how long a dried legume should be cooked; it is cooked when it is "done" to the tongue and tooth.

PREVENTING FLATULENCE

The only proven method for preventing flatulence is a commercial flavorless product that is sprinkled on the beans just before eating. The rest is up to the bacteria in each individual's stomach. Discarding the water has not been proven to reduce flatulence, no matter how much each of us claims it does to ease our concerns of social ostracism.

Butter Beans or Butter Peas

SERVES 4 TO 6

The constant stars of the Southern table, butter beans and the rounder butter peas are pale green in color, the size of a pencil eraser, and are delicate, moist, tender, and flavorful relatives of lima beans. Butter beans are known as sivvy beans in the Lowcountry and are eagerly awaited each summer. We buy butter beans in our farmers market in small sandwich-size plastic bags, already shelled and ready to use or freeze as they are. Commercially frozen butter beans and butter peas, as well as those called "white acres," are all very good substitutes for fresh, but avoid the lima bean–size brownish-tan ones for optimum flavor and texture. I love serving peas with Tomato Conserve (page 33), which is available in the grocery store in jars or is easy to make at home.

4 cups shelled fresh butter beans or butter peas

$1/4$ cup butter or bacon fat

$1/2$ small onion, sliced

Salt

Freshly ground black pepper

Bring enough salted water to the boil to cover the beans in a pot. Add the beans, butter, and onion. Return to the boil. Reduce heat, cover, and simmer 30 to 45 minutes, skimming off any foam as needed. Test to see if tender before draining. Season to taste with salt and pepper. Serve with the liquid if desired.

Variations:

• Add 2 teaspoons of chopped fresh lemon thyme, lemon balm, and basil.

• Add small baby carrots to the beans, along with 2 teaspoons of fresh herbs.

• Toss beans in some olive oil and serve with $1/3$ cup cooked fresh shrimp or drained canned tuna.

Green Beans

SERVES 4

Green beans are easily cooked ahead of time and reheated with any number of variations.

1 pound green beans, tipped, tailed, and stringed	Salt
2 tablespoons butter or oil	Freshly ground black pepper

Bring enough salted water to the boil to cover the beans. Add the beans and return to the boil. Reduce heat to medium and cook for 5 to 7 minutes, until the beans are no longer raw but still crisp. Drain and run under cold water to refresh and set the color. The beans may be made a day ahead and refrigerated or frozen at this point.

When ready to serve, heat the butter or oil to sizzling in a large frying pan. Add the beans and toss until heated through. Season to taste with salt and pepper.

Variations:

• Top the hot beans with Tomato Conserve (page 33) or warm Tomato Sauce (page 189).

• Toss with $1/2$ cup pecan halves.

• Sauté 1 pound of quartered or sliced mushrooms along with 4 chopped shallots or scallions in 4 tablespoons butter or oil for 1 to 2 minutes. Add the cooked green beans to the mushrooms and reheat. Add a tablespoon of chopped fresh herbs if desired.

• Toss with the grated rind of 1 lemon, no white attached.

• Toss with 1 teaspoon ground cumin or coriander seed and $1/2$ teaspoon sugar.

• Toss with 2 tablespoons sesame seeds or chopped pecans.

• Toss hot drained beans with Vibrant Vinaigrette (page 197). Toss just before serving. Serve warm or at room temperature.

• Top green beans with a mix of sliced roasted cherry, grape, or small tomatoes, and add sliced green or black olives, sautéed pecans, and/or crumbled goat cheese or other soft white cheese.

Pan-Charred Green Beans
with Tomato Conserve

Pan-Charred Green Beans

SERVES 4

Charred green beans were one of my first original recipes, when I only had a frying pan at hand and cooked them for a beau. They got neglected and we ate them slightly burned and loved them. Hence, charred green beans are a staple for us.

4 tablespoons butter

1 pound green beans, tipped, tailed, and stringed

Salt

Freshly ground black pepper

Melt the butter in a large frying pan. When very hot, add the beans and cook until dappled with dark brown, about 6 to 8 minutes. Reduce the heat, and continue cooking a few minutes more, stirring, until the beans are nearly soft. Season to taste with salt and pepper. Serve with Tomato Conserve.

Tomato Conserve or Preserve

MAKES 1 QUART

Also called tomato jam, this probable forerunner of ketchup may be purchased store-bought, but the homemade version is so much more enchanting that I had to start making my own. It is served atop vegetables of all sorts—beans and peas, greens, zucchini, eggplant, and others. Its earthy, deep-red color adds dimension wherever it goes. One woman wrote me recently that she also serves it with collards in a sandwich.

8 pounds fresh, ripe heirloom tomatoes, skinned, quartered, and seeded, or 4 (28-ounce) cans of tomatoes with juice

2 cups apple cider vinegar

1–1^{1}/$_{2}$ cups granulated sugar, divided

Salt

Freshly ground black pepper

Bring the tomatoes, vinegar, 1 cup sugar, and salt and pepper to taste to the boil in a heavy saucepan. Reduce heat and simmer until the mixture is thick enough to cling to a spoon, about 1^{1}/$_{2}$ to 2 hours, stirring so it does not burn. Taste and add some of the remaining sugar if desired. Cool and move to airtight containers, storing in the refrigerator for up to 2 to 3 weeks, or freeze for later use.

Crisp Pole Beans

In the last thirty years, it has become increasingly popular to eat pole beans in a modern way. We've found crisp garden-fresh pole beans in the summer are a yummy treat, blanched briefly to preserve their bright color and clean flavor. With garlic and shallots, the whole kitchen smells wonderful, and it's really hard to keep everyone's fingers out of the pan. Doubling the recipe is never a bad idea so that enough makes it to the table. The fat can be varied as desired.

1 pound pole beans, tipped, tailed, and stringed

1 tablespoon butter

1 tablespoon bacon drippings

1 large shallot, chopped

1 garlic clove, chopped

1 tablespoon chopped fresh thyme or other fresh herbs, optional

Salt

Freshly ground black pepper

Bring enough water to cover the beans to the boil in a large pot. Slice the beans on the diagonal into 2-inch pieces. Add beans to the boiling water and cook until crisp-tender, 5 to 7 minutes. Drain.

When ready to serve, heat the butter and drippings in a skillet over medium heat. Add the shallot and garlic, cooking for about 2 minutes. Toss in the blanched beans and cook until warmed through. Add herbs if desired. Season to taste with salt and pepper.

Traditional Pole Beans

SERVES 8 TO 10

These long, tough green beans, originally Kentucky Wonders, always need stringing. The traditional long-cooking method was probably derived to incorporate the fat into the beans as an important source of energy, as well as to make them palatable and flavorful. No vitamins are lost, as the broth is eaten too. They hold their shape, just barely.

2 ham hocks or ¼ cup white bacon, streak o' lean, or fatback, sliced (page 99)

2 pounds pole green beans, stringed and cut into 2-inch pieces

1 teaspoon granulated sugar, optional

1 medium onion, peeled

Salt

Freshly ground black pepper

Rinse the hocks or pork fat if necessary, and cover with water in a pot. Bring to the boil and cook for 30 minutes, skimming off the foam as needed. Remove the ham hocks from the pot of broth, add the green beans and more water if necessary to cover the beans, and return to the boil. Add sugar if desired. Put the ham hocks on top of the beans and add the whole onion to the pot. Bring to the boil, then reduce heat, taking care that the pork stays on top to melt and flavor the beans. Reduce the heat and simmer until very tender, about 1 to 1¹/₂ hours, skimming off the foam as needed. Season to taste with salt and pepper. If desired, remove the ham from the bones and serve it with the beans.

Variation: Charred Pole Beans

If possible, these are even more delicious that regular green beans when charred (see Pan-Charred Green Beans, page 33). After stringing, treat in the same way as asparagus or green beans.

Variations:

• Top the hot beans with 1 cup Tomato Conserve (page 33) or warm Tomato Sauce (page 189).

• Add 14 small scrubbed potatoes during the last 30 minutes of cooking.

• Try any of the variations under Green Beans (page 31)

REDUCING SCUM (FOAM)

When possible, liquid added to vegetables for further cooking should be near boiling. It shocks the vegetables and reduces the amount of vegetable scum.

Black-Eyed Peas with Hog Jowl

SERVES 6

The black-eyed pea isn't really a pea at all; it's a bean. Be that as it may, black-eyed peas are served all year long but with special emphasis to bring luck on New Year's Day. Combined with an equal amount of cooked rice, they make a traditional African dish, now called Hoppin' John, and form a complete protein—a vital source of food for what President Franklin D. Roosevelt called "the Shoeless South" during the Great Depression and other hard times.

1 pound dried black-eyed peas

¼–½ pound hog jowl, fatback, or other smoked meat

1 jalapeño or other small hot pepper, optional

Salt

Freshly ground black pepper

Pour boiling water over the dried peas or beans in a large pot and set aside. Meanwhile, make a broth by covering the hog jowl and optional pepper with water and bringing to the boil. Reduce heat and simmer for 1 hour to extract the juices and reduce the liquid, skimming off the foam as needed.

Pour off and discard the water from the peas. Pour the hog jowl broth over the peas; remove the jowl if desired. Simmer 30 minutes to 1 hour, or until peas are tender but still individuated, not mushy, skimming off any foam.

Variation: To use fresh or frozen black-eyed peas, cook the hog jowl as above. After 1 hour, add 2 pounds fresh or frozen peas and simmer as above.

Southern Hummus

MAKES 6 CUPS

New Southern chefs have taken to creating "Southern hummus." Any butter bean or pea can be used in this recipe, with the caveat that the canned beans and frozen beans will require less cooking than fresh and should be drained before using. Seasoning will always vary according to the bean, so the measurements are just a guideline. This dip is significantly better the next day.

2 pounds fresh or frozen butter beans, butter peas, or English peas

2 medium Vidalia or other onions, chopped

8 garlic cloves, smashed and peeled

1 tablespoon salt

1/4 cup chopped fresh cilantro

1/4 cup smooth peanut butter or tahini

2 teaspoons ground cumin seed

1/4 teaspoon ground hot red pepper

3 ounces freshly squeezed lemon juice

1/2 cup olive oil, divided

Salt

Freshly ground black pepper

Ground coriander seed

Quartered pita bread, other sturdy bread, or raw vegetables for dipping

Add the beans, onion, garlic, and salt to boiling water to cover in a large pot. Reduce heat to a simmer, cover, and simmer 10 to 20 minutes, or until beans are tender; skim off any foam as needed (page 36). Drain the skimmed bean mixture and move to a food processor bowl or strong blender. Add the cilantro, peanut butter, cumin, red pepper, lemon juice, and 1/3 cup oil. Purée until smooth. Season to taste with salt and pepper. This can be made several days in advance and refrigerated. Drizzle remaining oil on top just before serving, and sprinkle with coriander.

Serve with pita bread, raw vegetables, or crackers.

Variation: Add 1 teaspoon chopped fresh mint or dill.

Hoppin' John

Hoppin' John

A must-do dish at New Year's and other holidays, the peas represent good luck and health. Traditionally, since this was a New Year's dish, the peas were dried, but, of course, canned or frozen are readily substituted and seen nearly all year long. Two cups dried peas equals four to five cups fresh or frozen peas (with or without snaps). The preferred pea varies according to the region of the South and is debated by enthusiasts.

2 cups dried black-eyed peas, lady peas, or cowpeas

1 piece fatback, hog jowl, or other smoked meat, slashed in several places

1 hot red pepper

1 medium onion, chopped

Salt

Freshly ground black pepper

1 cup uncooked rice

4 tablespoons drippings, preferably bacon

Pour boiling water over the dried peas in a large pot and set aside while preparing other ingredients. When ready to proceed, drain the peas and discard the water. Add fresh water to cover the peas. Add the fatback, hot red pepper, onion, salt, and black pepper. Bring to the boil; cover, reduce heat, and simmer until the peas are nearly tender, 45 minutes to 1 hour, skimming off the foam as needed. Add more water as needed. Continue cooking, covered, until the peas are tender. Remove the peas with a slotted spoon, reserving 3 cups liquid in the pot.

Bring reserved liquid to the boil, add the rice, and return to the boil; cover. Reduce heat and simmer until the rice is cooked, about 20 to 30 minutes. Return peas to the pot, stir together, and cook for a few minutes more. Add drippings to flavor the dish, taste, and adjust seasonings. Serve hot or make into a tasty salad.

Variation: Add cooked frozen or drained canned black-eyed or crowder peas, and cooked bacon to cooked rice and heat together.

Mississippi Caviar

SERVES 25

This wonderful make-ahead dip is perfect for a large party. Made from black-eyed peas—the South's caviar—it can also be a vegetable bed for grilled or smoked chops. Cover and refrigerate for up to 4 or 5 days or freeze up to 3 months.

4 cups cooked and drained black-eyed peas

1/2 cup finely chopped green bell pepper

1/2 cup finely chopped red bell pepper

3/4 cup finely chopped hot peppers

3/4 cup finely chopped onion

1/4 cup drained and finely chopped pimento

1 garlic clove, chopped

1/3 cup red wine vinegar

2/3 cup olive oil

1 tablespoon Dijon mustard

Salt

Hot sauce

Combine the peas, bell peppers, hot peppers, onion, pimento, and garlic in a large bowl. Whisk together the vinegar, oil, and mustard, and pour over the bean mixture; mix well. Season to taste with salt and hot sauce. With a heavy wooden spoon, mash the bean mixture slightly. Refrigerate until ready to serve. Drain well before serving.

Fresh Crowder Peas with Snaps

SERVES 6

Crowder peas are a tougher small pea than white acres or lady peas. Even when green (fresh), they tend to be a drier pea than many others but burst with flavor. Like other zipper peas, it is a rare treat to find them shelled unless frozen or canned.

2 1/2 pounds fresh Crowder peas to yield
1 1/2 pounds shelled peas

3 ounces fatback (salt pork)

1 small hot red pepper, optional

Shell the peas and check for wormholes. If any pods are too tiny to shell, leave them whole or snap them in half. Cook these "snaps" with the shelled peas.

Bring enough water to cover the peas to the boil. Slice the fatback four times but leave it whole, with the rind intact. Add the slices to the boiling water along with the peas, snaps, and optional hot red pepper. Return to the boil, reduce heat, and simmer the peas for about 1 hour. Serve hot in the cooking liquid.

Lady Pea Patties

MAKES 24 SMALL PATTIES

Hands are enough implements for eating these tasty patties. Serve from the pan, stack on the buffet table, or pass with napkins. Any cooked peas can be made into a similar patty, so don't feel locked in to lady peas just because they are my favorite!

3 cups cooked and drained lady peas

1 large egg, lightly beaten

2–3 tablespoons chopped fresh thyme, basil, and/or oregano

1 small red onion, chopped

2 garlic cloves, chopped

1 green onion, or scallion, chopped

1/2 jalapeño pepper or other small hot pepper, roasted, peeled, seeded, and finely chopped

All-purpose flour

Shortening or vegetable oil for frying

Garlic and Red Pepper Mayonnaise (page 195)

Line a rimmed baking sheet with parchment or waxed paper and set aside.

Mash the peas with a fork in a large mixing bowl or pulse 3 or 4 times in a food processor. Mix in the egg, herbs, red onion, garlic, green onion, and desired amount of jalapeño pepper.

Form the mixture by hand into 24 small patties. Sprinkle the patties lightly with flour on both sides and move to prepared baking sheet.

Coat the bottom of a large skillet with oil and heat until shimmering. Cooking in batches, cook patties $1^1/2$ to 2 minutes on the first side. Turn with a spatula and cook another $1^1/2$ to 2 minutes on the second side. Remove to a warm serving platter.

Serve hot with Red Pepper Mayonnaise.

Throw-Together Corn and Field Pea Dip

MAKES 4 CUPS

Unique and very easy, this can be thrown together the night before the party or even an hour before to let the flavors meld. Fresh raw (green) corn, cooked corn, and canned kernels all work fine in this recipe.

2 cups cooked field peas with snaps, or 1 (15-ounce) can, rinsed and drained

1½ cups cooked corn or 1 (11-ounce) can white shoepeg corn, drained

½ cup peeled, seeded, and diced tomatoes

1 jalapeño pepper or other small hot pepper, seeded and finely chopped

¼ cup finely chopped onion

1 garlic clove, chopped

2 tablespoons chopped fresh parsley

¼ cup olive oil

¼ cup red wine vinegar

2 tablespoons freshly squeezed lemon juice

Salt

Tortilla chips or crackers

Toss the peas, corn, tomatoes, pepper, onion, garlic, and parsley in a bowl.

Whisk together oil, vinegar, and lemon juice. Pour over the pea mixture and toss. Season to taste with salt. Cover and refrigerate at least 1 hour or overnight.

Drain before serving with tortilla chips or crackers.

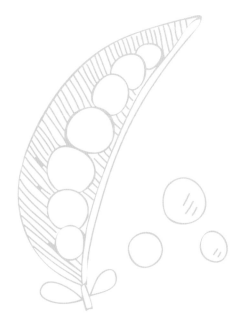

English (Green) Peas

SERVES 4

Green peas were brought from England to the New World and identified as part of English cooking merely by their name. Many people in other areas of the country call them green peas, although all peas have a "green," or raw, state. English peas are the most vibrant green of all peas and cook quickly. They have a sweetness when freshly picked and are eaten raw by many a cook while shelling them. Sugar is added by many cooks to keep English peas sweet. They freeze well when shelled.

1/2 cup chicken stock or broth, or water

2 cups shelled fresh or frozen English peas

5 tablespoons butter

Salt

Freshly ground black pepper

Granulated sugar, optional

Bring stock or water to the boil in a large saucepan. Add peas and butter, return to the boil, cover, and cook for 3 to 4 minutes. Drain. Season to taste with salt and pepper and optional sugar.

Variation: Peas with Wilted Lettuce

Add 1 tablespoon chopped fresh thyme, romaine lettuce, and 1 bunch roughly chopped green onions to the cooked peas; heat until lettuce is slightly wilted.

FROZEN PEAS

Commercially frozen peas need little if any further cooking. They are also unique in that the quick freezing done commercially traps the sugar inside and keeps them from losing flavor. Fresh English peas start to lose flavor quickly once picked.

Creamed English Peas and Potatoes

SERVES 4 TO 6

"Creamers" is the name for just-picked small potatoes. Combined with English peas and a cream sauce, they add a splendid touch to holiday or company meals, hence, "creamed" creamers and English peas. Use a large pot to prevent the potatoes from boiling over.

12 small creamers or fingerling potatoes	3 tablespoons all-purpose flour
2 cups shelled fresh English peas	1/2 cup heavy cream
8 tablespoons butter, divided	Salt
1 medium onion, sliced	Freshly ground black pepper

Peel a band around the potatoes with a swivel peeler or knife. Cut up any large potatoes so that none are larger than $1^1/_2$ inches in diameter. Rinse and add to a pot of boiling water to cover. Return to the boil, reduce to a simmer, and cook until the potatoes are tender when pierced with a fork, 20 to 30 minutes, depending on size. Add the peas and simmer 5 minutes more.

Meanwhile, heat 3 tablespoons of butter in a frying pan. Add the onion and sauté until tender, about 5 minutes.

Add the remaining 5 tablespoons butter to the pan. Stir in the flour to make a roux. Add heavy cream to the roux. Bring to the boil, stirring continuously to make a white sauce. Pour the sauce into the undrained potatoes and peas. Season to taste with salt and pepper.

BEETS

New varieties of beets in multiple colors shimmer on the plate—diced, julienned, grated, sliced, or quartered. The small ones can be appealingly sweet and are a delight when cooked crispy. Unfortunately, my husband doesn't like beets and before we were married made me promise never to serve them to him. What a shame.

In some countries, like France, beets are sold already cooked. Farmers boil them in pots in the field, saving the hapless home cook from being covered in red dye from head to toe, as often happens here.

Select beets that are firm. Cut off the greens immediately to prevent the beets from softening and losing flavor. Prepare and store the greens as you would other greens (page 97).

While cooking beet greens, add roasted and sliced beets back to their greens, which flavors both the beets and the greens.

Hot or Cold Roasted Beet Salad

Hot or Cold Roasted Beet Salad

SERVES 2

This is a basic beet salad dressed with a simple vinaigrette. The variations provide endless opportunities to enjoy fresh beets.

3 tablespoons red or white wine vinegar

2 tablespoons Dijon mustard

1 teaspoon granulated sugar

3 tablespoons oil

1 tablespoon finely chopped herbs, such as marjoram, thyme, or basil

4 medium roasted beets (page 48), preferably multicolored, peeled

Salt

Freshly ground black pepper

2 tablespoons chopped chives or green onion ends

Whisk together the vinegar, mustard, and sugar in a small bowl. While whisking, slowly drizzle in the oil and continue whisking until emulsified (page 193). Whisk in the herbs. Slice, quarter, or grate the beets, depending on size. Pour dressing over beets. Season to taste with salt and pepper. Refrigerate until chilled. Top with chives.

Variations:

• Add grated ginger.

• Place beets on a bed of lettuce, arugula, or chiffonade (page 100) of baby beet greens.

• Sprinkle with grated hard-cooked egg whites.

• Substitute small beets, barely roasted.

• Slice and layer with crumbled feta or blue cheese.

• Sprinkle with cooked salmon or tuna.

• Surround with cooked baby potatoes.

• Toss with orange slices.

• Omit vinaigrette and substitute sour cream.

PREVENTING BEET JUICE STAINS

Beet juice will stain anything and everything it comes into contact with—hands, cutting board, etc. Clear the work area of anything you don't want to stain vibrant red. Use plastic gloves and plastic cutting boards when cutting the beets.

Cut off the beet stem close to, but not into, the beet. As for the root, cut close to the beet but leave a short tail. Both of these cuts will prevent excess dye from escaping the beet.

Roasted Beets

SERVES 4

Baking beets in aluminum foil makes them easier to peel than boiling or steaming them. The roasting increases the flavor as well. They can be returned to the oven when peeled to roast and deepen in color.

4–6 medium beets

Preheat oven to 400 degrees.

Wrap beets in sturdy aluminum foil. Move the wrapped beets to a rimmed baking sheet and cook 1 hour, or until beets are tender. When beets are cool enough to handle, slip off peel. Serve as is, use in another recipe, or return to oven (unwrapped) to roast and deepen their color.

Variation: Beet Quarters with Lemon

After peeling, quarter the beets. Heat 2 tablespoons oil in a pan, add the beets, and toss until heated through. Add the juice of $1/2$ lemon. Season to taste with salt and pepper.

BROCCOLI

Broccoli is two vegetables in one: The crisp stalk may be cut horizontally in amoeba-like slices, vertically in fingers, grated like cole-slaw, or ribboned like zucchini. The crown, also called the flower, or head, contains delicate florets. Select firm heads with crisp stalks and avoid those that have begun to yellow. Store broccoli in the refrigerator, loosely wrapped in plastic.

If you can smell it, it is usually overcooked! Since the stalk and the florets are different thicknesses and textures, it is hard to get the whole thing cooked enjoyably unless part or all of the stem is removed. But don't throw it away—sometimes I cook the two together, the crunch of the stalk and the florets a contrast to each other. Other times I cook them in two different ways, served together or for separate meals. The little leaves hugging the broccoli are also delicious. Save them and sauté them too.

Broccoli Trees Slathered with Garlic

SERVES 4 TO 6

There is something so enticing about this manner of cooking broccoli; even children—particularly children—love it, and its name appeals to them.

1 head broccoli

1½ tablespoons butter

6–8 garlic cloves, peeled

Salt

Freshly ground black pepper

Cut the tough end of the stem off the broccoli, leaving the rest of stem attached to the florets. Cut the broccoli into florets down through the stem. Heat the butter over medium-high heat in a large skillet, add the garlic, and cook 3 to 5 minutes. Add the broccoli trees, spreading so they are in one layer. Cook 1 minute. Turn the trees carefully with tongs and cook an additional minute. Reduce heat to low, cover the pan, and cook broccoli 8 to 10 minutes. Uncover and cook until any moisture evaporates, another 3 to 5 minutes, and the stem is crisp-tender but still green. Season to taste with salt and pepper.

Variation: Add ¼ teaspoon turmeric or curry powder.

Variation: Roasted Broccoli Trees

Toss with 1 tablespoon oil and roast at 400 degrees for 10 to 15 minutes until tender crisp. Pan sauté garlic in butter.

Variation: Broccoli Steaks

These steaks also look like trees.

Cut stem off broccoli. Slice in half vertically from base to floret. Slice each half in half again. Cook or roast as above. Cauliflower may be prepared in the same fashion.

Broccoli Trees Slathered with Garlic

BROCCOLI SLAW

Sold in bags, as are other mixed slaws, it is a time-saver for a quick stir-fry and wilts easily in the pan.

Quick Braised Broccoli

SERVES 4

This recipe shows how to cook a green vegetable in advance and reheat it. It uses nearly all of the vegetable, cooked in a little water and butter. When I was young, my mother cooked green vegetables in a large quantity of boiling water, turning them to a yellowish mush. Crisp-cooking insures a full-bodied green vegetable.

1 head broccoli	Salt
4 tablespoons butter, divided	Freshly ground black pepper
2 garlic cloves, chopped	

Trim off the tough end of the broccoli stalk. Peel the rest of the stalk to just below the florets; cut the stalk off and slice $1/4$ inch thick. Alternatively, trim the stalk into a long rectangle, and then dice into pieces. Heat 2 tablespoons of butter in a frying pan, add the sliced stalks, and toss 3 minutes over high heat.

Meanwhile, break the head into florets. Add them to the pan, with or without stalks, with a few tablespoons water, cover, and cook 2 minutes more. This may be done up to a day in advance.

When ready to serve, heat the remaining butter in a frying pan, add the garlic, and cook briefly. Add the broccoli and toss over medium heat until coated with the garlic and butter. Season to taste with salt and pepper.

Variation: Add $1/2$ cup freshly grated Parmesan cheese to the frying pan when reheating the broccoli.

Variation: Broccoli Greens—If you are fortunate and grow your own, sauté the broccoli leaves.

Chopped Broccoli and Tomatoes

SERVES 4 TO 6

My houseguest Melissa introduced me to this. Chopping broccoli is an excellent way of encouraging everyone in the family to eat it. Braising it in a little liquid and adding tomatoes puts it over the top as a vegetable fit for entertaining as well. The broccoli may be chopped ahead and kept covered in the refrigerator for nearly a week.

1 head broccoli	10 grape tomatoes, halved
2 tablespoons butter or oil	Salt
1/2 cup chicken stock or broth, or water	Freshly ground pepper

Dry the cleaned broccoli, break into stalks, and slice off the tough ends and any leaves. Cut into pieces with a sharp knife and chop roughly but relatively uniformly. Heat the butter in a large skillet, add the broccoli, and stir-fry over medium heat for 2 to 3 minutes. Add the liquid, cover, and cook until broccoli is tender yet still crisp, about 2 to 3 minutes. Remove the lid, add the tomatoes, and boil down the liquid until nearly gone. Season to taste with salt and pepper. This may be done ahead of time. When ready to serve, toss over heat a few minutes more, until any accumulated liquid is gone, and serve hot.

Variation: Add crumbled bacon, strips of ham, cooked chicken tenders, chopped fresh ginger, or grated cheese.

Variation: Cook the stems as you would sliced carrots—sauté, ribbon, or make into coleslaw. They can also be sliced vertically or in coins and sautéed, or charred, either in a pan with hot oil, when they become nibble good, or roasted as would be done with asparagus.

Broccoli with Red
Pepper, Olives, and Feta

Broccoli with Red Pepper, Olives, and Feta

SERVES 4

This is quick when using leftover or frozen florets. Frozen florets need only be heated through, not precooked. Cauliflower may be done the same way.

2 tablespoons oil

4 garlic cloves, chopped

10 Greek or Italian black olives, pitted and vertically sliced

1 roasted red bell pepper (page 137), vertically sliced

1 tablespoon finely chopped fresh oregano

1 tablespoon finely chopped fresh parsley

1 head broccoli florets, cooked (page 52)

4 ounces feta or soft goat cheese, crumbled

Salt

Freshly ground black pepper

1 teaspoon grated lemon rind, no white attached

Heat the oil in a large skillet. Add the garlic and cook 1 minute. Add the olives and red pepper to the pan, sprinkle with oregano and parsley, and cook until heated through. When ready to serve, reheat the pan and add the cooked broccoli. Crumble the cheese over the broccoli and heat through. Season to taste with salt and pepper. Sprinkle with lemon rind and serve warm.

PITTING OLIVES

To pit olives, place on a cutting board and swack down on them once or twice using the flat side of a knife blade and a fist. The pits are then easily removed by hand.

BRUSSELS SPROUTS

Brussels sprouts are another vegetable that modern cooking methods have caused to soar in popularity. It's a good-for-you crucifer, and my rule of thumb is if you can smell it cooking, it's cooked too much. Remove immediately from the heat, no matter what method of cooking—poaching, sautéing, roasting, or grilling.

Purchase Brussels sprouts with dark green, tightly formed heads. Those with loose leaves or that have begun to turn yellow are not fresh. Store loosely wrapped in plastic for up to 3 or 4 days, refrigerated.

Traditional Brussels Sprouts

SERVES 6

These are a gratifying winter vegetable for us in the South and they are beautiful on the plant. The right way of cooking is to produce a tantalizing gem on the plate, lightly crunchy, without the bitter taste and mushy peel of an overcooked one.

Cutting an X in the bottom of the stem allows it to cook quickly, in keeping with the shorter time the leaves require. Peel off any tough or yellow leaves. Cut very large Brussels sprouts into quarters before cooking.

1 pound Brussels sprouts	Freshly ground black pepper
Salt	2–4 tablespoons butter or oil

Cut off the tough tip of the stem. Cut an X about $1/4$ inch deep in the remaining stem. Bring a deep pan of generously salted water to the boil. Add the Brussels sprouts, return to the boil, reduce heat, and cook until a knife will pierce the sprouts, about 3 to 5 minutes. Take care that they are still firm. Run under cold water to refresh; drain. Season to taste with salt and pepper. They may be kept at room temperature several hours or refrigerated, covered, for up to 2 days before heating and serving. When ready to serve, heat butter in a large skillet, and Brussels sprouts until through.

Variations:

• Brussels sprouts are particularly good with seeds, such as benne (sesame), or nuts, such as pine, pecans, and walnuts.

• The addition of raisins, dried cherries, and other sweet dried fruits is an extraordinary way to enhance Brussels sprouts. Add fruit to the sprouts when reheating.

• Substitute chicken or vegetable stock or broth for the water.

Variation: Brussels Sprouts, Apples, and Pecans

Use 2 to 3 cups boiling apple cider instead of water. Add a chopped tart apple and cook 1 minute, covered. Add the sprouts and cook up to 3 minutes more. Drain, reserving broth for another purpose if desired. If reheating, toss sprouts and apples in 2 tablespoons butter or olive oil until warmed through. Top with $1/3$ cup chopped pecans.

Sautéed Brussels Sprouts Leaves

Sautéed Brussels Sprouts Leaves

SERVES 6

What a miracle these little leaves are when sautéed quickly in butter or oil.

1 pound Brussels sprout leaves	Salt
2–4 tablespoons butter or oil	Freshly ground black pepper

Heat the butter or oil in a large frying pan. Add the Brussels sprouts leaves and sauté quickly over medium heat until they wilt, about 2 minutes. Season to taste with salt and freshly ground pepper.

Variation: Slice the sprouts thinly, removing as much of the stem as possible, and follow the directions for sautéing.

Variation: Charred Brussels Sprouts

Cut in half, toss in oil, and put cut side down on grill. Remove when charred as desired.

REMOVING BRUSSELS SPROUT STEMS

Peel off the leaves from the outside and discard the stems. Or remove the stem with a knife and slice the sprouts. Or use a small sharp knife to cut a circle around the stem and remove it by digging inside the sprout. With two fingers, open the sprout and separate the leaves.

CABBAGE

Winter varieties of cabbage produce the firm, heavy heads most of us recognize. The summer varieties are sweeter and have more open leaves, producing a lighter head. Overcooking is the usual mistake, so keep the cooking times short.

Select green or red cabbages with either firm heads or more open leaves, depending on the season as above. Cabbage stores for weeks refrigerated. Remove any loose or wilted leaves before preparing.

REMOVING CABBAGE CORE

Forceful people can remove the core by whacking the stem end of the whole head sturdily on the edge of a counter. The more timid of us remove the core with a knife after cutting the cabbage into wedges.

FREEZING CABBAGE

Cabbage seems so small when still a head. Cut or shredded, it becomes abundant and generous, the parts much greater than the whole. If too abundant to use up in a short time, slice and blanch all of it and freeze a portion for a later time.

Simple Cabbage

SERVES 6 TO 8

The phrase "cabbage-and-cornbread" is spoken as one word, as that is the way cabbage is most often served—with crumbled cornbread in a bowl or sandwiched in cornbread. Still, it is very tasty served with meats and other vegetables. I so enjoy eating and serving it with the "pot likker." I still serve it in a bowl rather than on a plate, so everyone can have some of the broth.

1 head green or red cabbage, about 6 inches in diameter

2 cups water

1/2 cup butter

Salt

Freshly ground black pepper

Cut the cabbage into 6 to 8 wedges and remove the core. Bring water to the boil and add the cabbage and butter. Cover tightly with a lid, reduce heat, and simmer for 15 to 20 minutes, until the cabbage is tender but has a little give. There should be 1 cup or so of water left in the pot. Season to taste with salt and pepper. Serve the cabbage with the liquid.

Variations:

• Slice cabbage 1/3 inch thick. Sauté 1 onion in a few tablespoons of oil and add to the uncooked cabbage. Bring enough water to cover the cabbage to the boil. Add the cabbage and onions, cover, reduce heat, and simmer for 15 to 20 minutes. Transfer the cabbage with a slotted spoon to a plate or bowl. Boil the "pot likker" sufficient to reduce the liquid down to about 1/2 cup. Garnish with chopped thyme or oregano.

• Top drained cabbage with Tomato Conserve (page 33).

Variation: Grilled Cabbage

To grill, cool cooked cabbage quarters sufficient to be able to handle them. Pat dry. Brush on all sides with oil and move to a hot grill. Cook about 10 minutes per side, checking to see that they do not burn. Season to taste with salt and pepper. Sprinkle with optional vinegar just before serving.

Sautéed Cabbage

SERVES 2

The flavor that comes from quickly sautéing cabbage and braising it in butter and cream is incredibly full and rich. There is a small chance an iron skillet will flavor the cream, so use a non-iron variety.

3 tablespoons butter

½ medium green cabbage, cored and cut into ¼-inch strips

Salt

Freshly ground black pepper

Heat the butter in a large, heavy, non-iron frying pan over medium heat. Add the cabbage and sauté for 5 minutes, tossing to coat the cabbage with the butter. Cook the cabbage another 5 minutes, tossing occasionally. Season to taste with salt and pepper. Serve immediately.

Variation: Creamed Sautéed Cabbage

Add ½ cup heavy cream after the first 5 minutes of cooking. Bring quickly to the boil, cover the pan, and reduce the heat. Cook the cabbage over low heat for 15 minutes, or until tender but not mushy. Season to taste with salt and pepper. Sprinkle with 1 teaspoon chopped fresh tarragon (optional) before serving.

Wilted Coleslaw for a Crowd

SERVES 10 TO 15

Coleslaw entered the American food scene in the Dutch colonies (from the Dutch koolsla, a combination of kool, "cabbage," and sla, "salad") and has nearly as many variations as there are cooks. From early Roman times, coleslaw has been prepared with a vinegar base, and only in the last 200 years or so did the mayonnaise varieties begin to appear. It seems every Southerner has his or her own recipe and way of cutting the cabbage. In this recipe, the cabbage wilts when the hot dressing is added.

4–5 pounds green or red cabbage

2–3 large Vidalia or other sweet onions, chopped

1½ cups oil

1 cup apple cider vinegar

1 tablespoon Dijon mustard

1 tablespoon–1 cup granulated sugar

Prepare cabbage as desired—shredded, chopped, sliced, or grated. Toss the cabbage and onions together in a large bowl.

Bring the oil, vinegar, mustard, and preferred amount of sugar to the boil in a saucepan. Pour the dressing over the cabbage. Chill, stirring from time to time.

Variations:

• Add chopped or grated carrots.

• My friend Elliot Mackle adds ¹/₂ teaspoon caraway seed per cabbage and uses less onion.

PREPARING CABBAGE

Chopped—Halve or quarter the cabbage and process in a food processor until desired size. To chop by hand, cut into thin slices, and then move knife rapidly over slices until desired size.

Finely chopped—Process quarters of the cabbage in a food processor or other machine until very fine.

Grated—Halve or quarter the cabbage and carefully rub on a grater, watching knuckles.

Shredded—Halve or quarter the cabbage and slice down with a sharp knife at the desired thickness.

COMMERCIAL MAYONNAISE FOR COLESLAW

Homemade mayonnaise is discouraged in all slaw recipes because it is easily diluted as the cabbage weeps. This dilutes the acid in the mayonnaise, which acts as the preservative for the egg in the mayonnaise. In a commercial mayonnaise product, the eggs are processed and therefore still have preservative properties.

Traditional Coleslaw

SERVES 10 TO 15

The diversity in coleslaw comes from the size of the cabbage pieces; it's very finely machine chopped for cafeterias and schools, and we've all gotten to like it on top of barbecue on a bun. Halved and quartered before slicing thickly, makes it more rustic and adds a homemade feeling, sort of "grandmother loves me." And sliced thinly is like a gourmet chef is cooking in your kitchen. Using commercial mayonnaise enables making this dish several days in advance. Some people salt, rinse, and drain the cabbage before using, to reduce the tendency of the cabbage to release water.

4 pounds green or red cabbage, sliced, grated, or shredded (page 63)

2 Vidalia or other sweet onions, finely chopped

1½ cups mayonnaise, preferably store-bought

Dijon mustard

Salt

Freshly ground black pepper

Cider vinegar

Toss the cabbage with the onions and mayonnaise; taste. Add mustard, salt, and pepper as desired. Add a little cider vinegar for a zesty flavor.

Variations:

• Add grated carrots.

• Add a bit of hot red pepper.

• Crown with chopped salted peanuts.

CARROTS

Once upon a time, "carrot-colored" described an orange root vegetable. Now, carrots are coming out of the ground crimson, beige, bronze, and tinged with green. They can be reed thin or finger size and stubby. They only need a little scraping rather than a vigorous peeling. They are sweet and delicious eaten raw or cooked.

When purchasing "baby carrots," check the label. A true Baby Carrot, bred to be small, will be labeled as such. Most packaged "baby carrots" will state that they are "baby-cut carrots," or larger carrots cut down to a uniform small size.

Store carrots loosely wrapped in plastic up to two weeks in the refrigerator.

The time needed to cook carrots varies according to their age and thickness. Baby carrots, by their very tenderness, cook more quickly. Older carrots are tougher, and their center core requires longer cooking. Older root vegetables should go into cold water, baby carrots into boiling water.

Glazed Baby Carrots

SERVES 4 TO 6

This family-friendly vegetable has dozens of variations. The sugar sweetens the carrots depending on size as well as giving the carrots an appealing gloss.

1 pound baby carrots

2–4 tablespoons butter or oil, divided

1 tablespoon granulated sugar or honey

Salt

Freshly ground black pepper

Scrape the carrots and remove roots. Add to a frying pan of boiling salted water only to cover. Add 1 tablespoon butter or oil and sugar. Cook 2 to 3 minutes, until crisp-tender. Uncover and boil the liquid until it becomes a glaze. Add remaining butter or oil as desired. Season to taste with salt and pepper.

Variations:

• Add chopped herbs such as thyme or parsley.

• Add a teaspoon of finely chopped or grated ginger.

Sautéed Grated Carrots

SERVES 4

Carrots and root vegetables are the answer to winter vegetable doldrums. This manner of cooking them promises of spring and is particularly suited to full-sized carrots. The optional ginger addition is a favorite of mine.

6 carrots	Salt
1 tablespoon butter	Freshly ground black pepper
1–2 tablespoons chopped ginger, optional	

Remove any greens and the stem end of the top, and peel the carrots. Put through the grating blade of a food processor or grate by hand. Melt the butter in a large skillet over medium-high heat. Add the optional ginger and grated carrots, and cook, stirring constantly, until the carrots are crisp-tender and have lost their raw taste, about 3 to 5 minutes. Season to taste with salt and pepper. Can be made ahead and reheated.

Variation: Sautéed Honey-and-Orange Carrots

Add the grated rind of 1 orange, no white attached, $1/3$ cup honey, and $1/3$ cup red wine vinegar to the cooked gingered carrots. Toss over medium heat until heated through.

Variation: Add an equal amount of grated zucchini halfway through.

OUCHLESS GRATED CARROTS

Along with food processors and graters, there are many fancy graters available to grate vegetables, so scout yard sales and cookware stores. If a box grater is the only thing available, use a soft plastic bag over the grating hand to preserve knuckles.

Ribboned Carrots and Zucchini

Ribboned Carrots and Zucchini

SERVES 2 TO 3

Ribboned vegetables are paper-thin strips of firm vegetables such as beets, carrots, zucchini, turnips, and potatoes. One of their many virtues is that ribbons cook faster than almost any other shape of cut vegetables, except finely chopped. They may be cooked ahead and even used for a salad. This technique is particularly useful when there are stray vegetables in the bin. Vegetables may be ribboned in advance and kept refrigerated for several days until ready to cook.

1 tablespoon butter or oil

1–2 carrots

1–2 zucchini

1 tablespoon chopped fresh thyme, rosemary, or other favorite herb, optional

Salt

Freshly ground black pepper

Melt the butter in a frying pan. Ribbon the vegetables with a potato peeler. Reserve one long exterior strip of zucchini for each serving. Add the ribbons to the hot pan. Cover with a lid and cook 1 to 3 minutes. Remove lid, season to taste with herbs, salt, and pepper. Take each of the reserved zucchini strips and form into individual rings. Divide cooked ribbons equally between the rings, piling them inside the rings. Serve immediately, or cool and reheat later.

Variation: Add sliced mushrooms and ribboned turnips, potatoes, fennel, beets, and/or rutabagas if desired.

Variation: Substitute broccoli for all or some of the carrots.

RIBBONING

Ribboned (also called shaved) vegetables are delicious raw, tossed with Parmesan or goat cheese, olive oil, and a touch of sherry vinegar or lemon juice. Peel the vegetable vertically with a good vegetable peeler or mandoline, resulting in long, slender strips of vegetables that frequently curl when sliced so thinly. I include the seeds of zucchini and summer squash because I don't want to lose the nutrients.

CAULIFLOWER

Cauliflower is a cold-weather vegetable, although it is available year-round in our markets. The varieties found in the summer produce smaller heads but are often tastier. Look for firm, dense heads. Any slight discoloration can be cut off. Prevent raw cauliflower from turning brown by storing it in the refrigerator, stem side up, in an open plastic bag; poke a few holes in the bag so air can circulate. Or turn stem side down in a container of water.

Cauliflower Rice

SERVES 4 TO 6

A very versatile component of any meal, Cauliflower Rice can be used just like rice or couscous as a base for many recipes. Substitute with abandon. You may be pleasantly surprised.

1 head cauliflower (about 2 pounds)	Freshly ground black pepper
2 tablespoons olive oil	Freshly chopped herbs, optional
Salt	

Cut cauliflower into florets and add to food processor fitted with the metal blade. Pulse intermittently until cauliflower resembles rice. Heat olive oil over medium heat in a large sauté pan. Add cauliflower bits and toss in the oil. Season to taste with salt and pepper. Cook 6 to 8 minutes, until cauliflower is softened and lightly browned. Serve as a base as you would with rice, or alone with chopped fresh herbs.

Mashed Cauliflower

Cauliflower and other cruciferous vegetables, like broccoli, are finally entering their own and have become popular enough to warrant a variety of preparations, such as mashing. Very tasty in their own right, they are good combined with mashed potatoes or as a substitute for mashed potatoes. It's a good use for cauliflower that has been languishing in the refrigerator and has lost its pizzazz. The recipe can be adjusted as needed according to the amount of cauliflower available.

1 head cauliflower	Salt
2 tablespoons butter	Freshly ground pepper
½–1 cup milk, cream or broth	

Cut or snap off the florets from the stems. Chop the florets and add to a pan of boiling water, salted if desired, and cook until soft enough to mash. (The smaller the chop, the less time it takes to cook, from 15 to 30 minutes depending on size). Drain. Melt the butter in the drained pan. Heat the liquid separately in the microwave or another pan. Add the soft cauliflower florets to the pan with the butter and use a potato masher or other implement to mash them over low heat until they are the consistency of mashed potatoes, slowly adding as much liquid as necessary. These may be reheated in the microwave or over low heat.

Variation: Add mashed potatoes as desired to change consistency.

Cauliflower and Cheese Sauce

Cauliflower and Cheese Sauce

SERVES 4 TO 6

Crisp bits of buttered crumbs top the luscious cheese sauce cloaking the cauliflower. Fit for a king, this cheers up any dreary cold day. If possible, flavor the milk (page 74) for the cheese sauce.

1 head cauliflower (about 2 pounds)

2 tablespoons butter

1/3 cup breadcrumbs or panko

Cheese Sauce (recipe follows)

1/4 cup grated Cheddar cheese

Preheat oven to 350 degrees.

To cook the cauliflower, cut off the thick or discolored parts of the stem, removing all but the smallest green leaves. Make an X with a sharp knife in the remaining core, or remove core completely. (If the cauliflower is large, remove florets from the stem, discard stem, and cook florets in boiling water.) Move the whole cauliflower, stem side down, to a steamer basket over 1 cup of water. Cover and steam until tender, about 15 minutes. If microwaving, move to a microwave container, sprinkle with 2 tablespoons water, cover, and microwave until done, about 5 minutes. Drain.

Move the well-drained cauliflower to a heatproof serving bowl with the florets up. Sauté the breadcrumbs in the butter until brown. Top the cauliflower with the Cheese Sauce and the grated Cheddar cheese.

The recipe may be made ahead to this point. When ready to serve, move the dish to the hot oven until the cauliflower is heated through, the cheese is melted, and the sauce is light brown and bubbling. Top with browned breadcrumbs.

Cheese Sauce

MAKES ABOUT 2 CUPS

2 tablespoons butter

2 tablespoons all-purpose flour

1 1/2 cups milk, preferably flavored, page 74

1–3 teaspoons Dijon mustard

1/2 cup grated Cheddar cheese

Salt

Freshly ground black pepper

Melt butter in a medium saucepan and stir in the flour. Add the milk and stir the mixture until it comes to the boil. Remove from the heat and add the mustard and $^1/_2$ cup cheese. Stir until smooth and season to taste with salt and pepper.

Variation: Whole Cauliflower with Curry Sauce

Prepare cauliflower as above. Stir in 2 teaspoons curry powder with the flour and whisk 2 minutes, until smooth. Steam cauliflower as above and drain. Move to a food processor or blender with 3 ounces cream cheese. Process or blend until desired consistency.

Flavored Milk

MAKES 1 TO 2 CUPS

Any time milk is used in a savory recipe—from a white sauce to a quiche or soufflé—it is worth taking a little extra effort to flavor the milk. It enhances the end product immensely. Add bits and pieces as in a brown stock, using anything in the refrigerator that would enhance the flavor. Even onion and carrot peels can be used to flavor the milk. Do take care with celery leaf, as it is very strong and can dominate.

1–2 cups milk	1 slice fennel bulb, optional
1 slice onion	Peppercorns as desired
1 slice celery	Thyme, parsley stalk, as desired
1 slice carrot	

Heat milk in a saucepan or a glass measuring cup in the microwave with any of or all of the ingredients until warm and nearly at a simmer. Remove from heat and allow to sit for 30 minutes at room temperature, or longer in the fridge. Strain before using.

CELERY

Frequently used only as an accent in salads, soups, and stews, celery is overlooked as a vegetable. It can step into service nicely, particularly when the storage bin is bare.

Celery and Olive Salad

SERVES 2

This crisp, refreshing salad is a surprisingly remarkable addition to any table for so little effort and investment. It is adapted from Kim Sunee's Trail of Crumbs.

1–2 ribs celery	Salt
2–3 kalamata or French black olives	Freshly ground black pepper
2–3 tablespoons olive oil, divided	

Remove tough celery strings with a knife or scrape off with a peeler. Place the celery rib flat side down and slice on the diagonal as thinly as possible.

Cut the olives off the pit in small pieces. Toss together with 1 to 2 tablespoons olive oil, adding more oil as needed. Season to taste with salt and pepper. Serve chilled.

Variation: Add 1 teaspoon grated orange rind, no white attached.

Almost-Steamed Vegetables

Almost-Steamed Vegetables

SERVES 2 TO 3

This recipe affords the table color and dash when the larder is discouraging. In fact, this is a favorite way to serve vegetables all winter in my home. Cooked long on low heat, the vegetables extrude their own juices and are soft and tender. Cooked quickly, they are crisp. It's a long way from the dreadful canned or frozen peas and carrots of the 1950s that my family ate. It's hard to remember sometimes that carrots, much less peas, were not always available fresh year-round.

2 tablespoons butter	Salt
1 medium onion, thinly sliced	Freshly ground black pepper
1 carrot, thinly sliced	Herbs, as desired
1 celery rib, thinly sliced	

Heat a saucepan with the butter and add the onion, carrot, and celery. Season with salt and pepper. Cover and cook over low heat until the vegetables are cooked. Add herbs as desired.

Variation: Gingered Vegetable Medley

Heat $1^1/_2$ tablespoons butter or oil in a large frying pan until hot. Add 1 tablespoon finely chopped fresh ginger and cook 1 to 2 minutes. Add 1 julienned or grated carrot and 1 julienned or grated white turnip to the ginger and cook 2 to 3 minutes, until just beginning to soften. Add 2 julienned or grated zucchini and cook 2 to 3 minutes more. Stir to mix well. Season to taste with salt and pepper.

Variation: Glazed Carrots and Celery with Ginger

Melt 2 tablespoons butter in a heavy pan. Add 4 cups diagonally sliced carrots, 4 diagonally sliced celery ribs, and 2 teaspoons chopped fresh ginger. Cover and cook over low heat until crisp-tender. Add $1/_4$ cup sugar to the pan and stir slowly and gently until the carrots and celery are well glazed and slightly browned. Top with $1/_4$ cup fresh mint or parsley leaves.

CORN

America's rich history with corn began with Native Americans, who cooked corn by roasting it in ashes until the kernels were brown and then pounded the kernels into flour or processed the kernels with water mixed with ashes (lye water) to remove the hulls for whole hominy, which was later ground. The parched corn kept indefinitely and was mixed with hot or cold water and used as needed for cooking. Today, corn is ubiquitous—from fresh corn on the cob, to high-fructose corn syrup in processed foods, to feed for farm animals.

Farm-fresh corn is practically indescribable in its taste, and it's well worth running straight home to place it in boiling water. Purchase ears with their husks still on. Feel through the husk to confirm the kernels are plump. Store ears loosely wrapped in plastic in the refrigerator. Newer varieties of corn are bred to stay sweeter once picked, so refrigerated corn lasts several days.

Fresh corn can be microwaved, as below, shucked, and frozen flat on a rimmed baking sheet. When frozen, move to a plastic ziplock bag and use as you would commercial frozen corn. The corn may also be cut from the cob and frozen in the same fashion.

CORN ON THE COB

Freshly cooked corn on the cob is a treat. Pulling it off the cob gives a little crunch to the teeth, a flush of sweetness on the tongue, and a feeling of satisfaction when finished. In some countries it is street food. There are 800 kernels of corn on the average cob. Here are four spectacular ways to cook corn on the cob:

1. **Boiling corn on the cob**—Traditionally, corn on the cob is pre-shucked (removed from its husk and silks discarded), cooked in boiling water to cover until done (approximately 5 minutes once the water returns to the boil), drained, and served with butter, salt, and pepper.

2. **Microwaved corn on the cob**—This method is clearly the easiest and, to me, the corniest-tasting method of cooking corn. Microwave up to four ears of corn, with husk and silks

intact, on a glass pie plate or other shallow plate that will hold the corn easily. Cooking time is dependent on the quantity in the microwave. A little judicious testing is needed. Use 3 minutes per ear of corn for up to four ears as the guide. Remove from the microwave and let sit a few minutes in the husks until cool enough to handle. Pull the husks back but do not remove from the cob. Use a sturdy paper towel to pull the silks off the cob. Discard the silks. Leave the husks on as a "handle," or discard if preferred. Serve with butter, salt, and pepper.

3. Baked Corn on the Cob in the Husk—Preheat oven to 400 degrees. Soak the corn in its silk and husks in a shallow pan of water for 15 minutes. Spread the corn one layer deep on a rimmed baking sheet. Cook in the oven 45 minutes. Remove husks and silks carefully with a mitt or several layers of paper towel as above. Serve with butter, salt, and pepper.

4. Grilled Corn—Remove most of the husk from the cobs, leaving the last layer (where the kernels are visible through the husk). Cut off any silks from the end of the cob. Grill over medium heat for a total of 8 to 10 minutes, turning every 1 to 2 minutes.

REMOVING CORN FROM COBS

To scrape and milk the corn, hold a shucked ear of corn on its end in a shallow bowl or pie dish. Using a saw-ing motion, slice the tips of the corn kernels from the cob with a sharp knife, turning as needed. Slice down a second time to remove all the corn and its milk. Our friend Joe Yonan cuts the cob in half crosswise and places the cut side down in the dish. The cob is more stable that way.

To remove the remaining corn and "milk" next to the cob, use the blunt side of a knife to press and scrape down against the cob, turning as needed. Repeat with each ear of corn.

Easy Corn and Squash Pudding

SERVES 6 TO 8

Both corn and squash puddings are comfort foods craved at family and holiday meals. The combination of the two is suited to cure whatever ails both the able-bodied and the sick. A spoonful of corn pudding is practically medicinal in its power to restore. This dish does need a fair amount of salt. To taste before baking, heat a small portion in a pan or microwave and adjust salt as desired.

5 ears corn, shucked

3 slices bacon, cooked crisp and crumbled, drippings reserved

1 onion, chopped

3 garlic cloves, chopped

1 pound squash, such as summer yellow squash or zucchini

2 egg yolks

2 large whole eggs

$1/2$ cup milk

$1/2$ cup heavy cream

Salt

Freshly ground black pepper

$1/8$ teaspoon freshly ground nutmeg

1–2 teaspoons finely chopped fresh thyme

1 cup grated Gruyère cheese

Preheat oven to 375 degrees.

Remove corn kernels from the cobs with a sharp knife as described at left. Heat 2 tablespoons reserved drippings in a heavy skillet. Add the onion to the drippings and sauté, stirring as needed, until soft, 3 to 4 minutes. Add the garlic and sauté 1 minute. Cut the squash into $1/8$-inch-thick rounds. Add the corn and squash slices, cover, and cook until soft and wilted, about 10 minutes.

Whisk the yolks, the whole eggs, milk, cream, salt, pepper, nutmeg, and thyme together in a large bowl until smooth. Add the cheese, bacon, and the corn-and-squash mixture. Stir until well blended. Pour into a $2^1/2$-quart buttered casserole dish. Set the casserole in a shallow pan and pour $1/2$ inch of boiling water into the pan. Bake the casserole in the water bath for 45 to 50 minutes, or until the pudding is set in the center.

Easy Corn and Squash Pudding

Creamed or Fried Corn

SERVES 4 TO 6

Called either "fried" (since it's stewed in an iron skillet) or "creamed" (the starch from the corn milk makes a rich, thick, creamy dish), this is the quintessential home method of serving corn, as the liquid extracted is very flavorful, if scanty. Any leftovers can be reheated in the microwave or on top of the stove, or added to soup, grits, or another dish. The newer tender sweet corn varieties combined with bacon fat and butter are fantastic though decadent.

4–5 ears corn, shucked

2 slices thick-cut country bacon, cut into thin strips

1/2 cup water

4 tablespoons butter

Salt

Freshly ground black pepper

Remove corn kernels from the cobs with a sharp knife and scrape the milk as described on page 80.

Heat a 9- or 10-inch iron skillet or heavy frying pan and add the bacon. Cook carefully over medium heat, stirring as necessary, until crisp. Remove with a slotted spoon to a plate lined with a paper towel, leaving the drippings in the pan. Add the corn with its milk to the pan of bacon drippings along with the water. Bring to the boil, stirring. Add the butter and salt, and turn down to low heat. Cook, stirring frequently, about 20 to 30 minutes. Add more water if necessary. Perfect fried corn should be thick and sticky. Season to taste with salt and pepper. Garnish with crumbled bacon.

Variation: Meri's Creamy Corn

Add 1 diced white onion to the bacon drippings and sauté before adding the corn. Once the corn has cooked down, add 1/2 cup heavy cream to make a creamy sauce.

Variations:

• Omit the bacon and its fat and use butter.

• Add one chopped tomato and season with 1 tablespoon chopped fresh herbs.

• Add grilled shrimp or scallops.

• For New-Style Fried Corn, substitute butter for the bacon and stir-fry corn briefly. Add herbs if desired.

Maque Choux

Cajun and Creole cooks use everything in their larder to great advantage. Pronounced "mock shoe," this is an exciting and colorful addition to the table and uses everything in season.

6 ears corn, shucked

4 tablespoons butter

1 medium onion, chopped

2 garlic cloves, chopped

1 red or green bell pepper, cored, seeded, and chopped (or ½ of each color)

1 tomato, seeded and chopped

Salt

Freshly ground black pepper

Slice the tips of the corn kernels from the cob with a sharp knife as described on page 80.

Melt butter in a large frying pan or cast-iron skillet. Add onion, garlic, and bell pepper; sauté over medium heat, stirring as necessary, until soft. Add corn and tomato, and continue cooking until heated through and corn is crisp-tender, about 3 to 5 minutes. Season to taste with salt and pepper.

Variation: Add cooked shrimp or crab to the finished dish.

Summer Succotash

Summer Succotash

SERVES 6 TO 8

Cajuns make Maque Choux (page 83); elsewhere, we make succotash. While these dishes are similar, made with bacon drippings, sweet corn, peppers, and onions, Charlestonians add fresh butter beans, black-eyed peas, or other green field peas. Any fresh summer veggies enhance a succotash, so experiment. If there aren't any bacon drippings by the stove, use a mixture of butter and oil to sauté the vegetables.

1 pound fresh butter beans and/or other green field peas

1 medium onion, chopped and divided

Salt

2 tablespoons bacon or sausage drippings, or butter and oil

1 shallot, thinly sliced

2 garlic cloves, chopped

1 squash or zucchini, cut into 1/2-inch cubes

2 ears corn

Freshly ground black pepper

Bring enough salted water to the boil to cover the beans in a pot. Add beans and 1/2 of the chopped onion and return to the boil. Salt as needed. Reduce heat and simmer until beans are tender, 30 to 45 minutes, skimming off any foam as needed. Drain.

Heat drippings in a large skillet over medium heat; sauté shallot and remaining 1/2 onion until onion is translucent, about 10 minutes. Add garlic and sauté until fragrant, 2 to 3 minutes. Stir in squash and cook, stirring occasionally, until tender.

Slice the corn kernels from the cob with a sharp knife as described on page 80, reserving the cobs for another use (Corncob Stock, page 87). Add kernels, cooked butter beans, and fresh herbs to the squash. When ready to serve, cook, stirring occasionally, until just heated through, the corn still a bit crispy. Season to taste with salt and pepper. Refrigerate, covered, for 3 days or freeze for up to 3 months.

Variation:

Add 1/4 cup chopped fresh herbs and 1 cup sautéed mushrooms.

All peas are "green" before they become dry. Use them cooked or uncooked.

Corn and Butter Bean Salad

SERVES 6 TO 8

An ode to the summer garden, this salad brings amazing flavor to the table. Using fresh vegetables is always preferable; but sometimes the winter is long and I long for this succotash, so I bow to using frozen vegetables.

1 pound shelled butter beans or butter peas, fresh or frozen

6 ears corn on the cob, preferably Silver Queen, kernels scraped from the cob

1 green onion, or scallion, sliced, white and green parts

8 slices bacon, cooked crisp and crumbled

¾ cup mayonnaise

4 tablespoons white wine vinegar

3–4 tablespoons chopped fresh thyme, optional

Salt

Freshly ground black pepper

Add the butter beans to boiling salted water, reduce heat, and cook about 3 minutes. Add the corn and cook 1 minute more. Drain the beans and corn and run under cold water to stop the cooking and refresh them. Drain thoroughly.

Gently toss together the beans, corn, onion, bacon, mayonnaise, vinegar, and thyme. Season to taste with salt and pepper.

Cover with plastic wrap and refrigerate at least 1 hour before serving for the best marriage of flavors.

Variation: Substitute 1 (1-pound) package frozen white shoepeg corn or other whole kernel corn.

Corncob Stock

When eight or so corncobs are available, make this light, flavorful stock to use in chowders and soups. It freezes well for at least 3 months. For more flavor, use chicken or vegetable stock in lieu of water. The resulting broth may be boiled down to increase the flavor for a sauce or a smaller soup recipe.

8–10 corn cobs (kernels have been removed for another use)

1 medium onion, chopped

2 large carrots, chopped

6 –8 sprigs fresh thyme

1 teaspoon salt

Freshly ground black pepper

Move ingredients to a large stockpot. Add 3 to 4 quarts of water and bring to the boil. Reduce heat to simmer and cook stock about 45 minutes. Strain the stock, discarding the cobs and vegetables. Cool and use within a day or two, or freeze.

CUCUMBERS

Cucumbers are available year-round, but they really shine in the summer months, offering a cool, fresh flavor and crunch to salads and other dishes. Look for cucumbers that are firm, lacking any soft spots. Store cucumbers in the refrigerator for up to about a week, loosely wrapped in plastic wrap. Wrinkling or yellowing is a sign of a cucumber beginning to dry out, so avoid those if possible.

Perhaps it is just in my mind, but I do think raw cucumber that has had some of its juices removed by salting makes cucumbers rest easier in older tummies. We love them, but it doesn't seem to be a mutual feeling.

Cucumber Salad

SERVES 4

Cucumber salad is cooling to look at, as well as to eat. Traditionally, Southern cucumber salads are dressed with apple cider vinegar or plain vinegar and served in a glass or crystal dish all summer long.

SEEDING A CUCUMBER

Run a teaspoon down the center of the cucumber half, scraping away the seeds. A crescent shape will emerge when the cucumber is sliced.

2 cucumbers, peeled and thinly sliced

Salt

4 tablespoons granulated sugar

½ cup apple cider vinegar

2 green onions or scallions, chopped

2 tablespoons sesame seeds

Move the cucumber slices to a colander placed over a bowl or sink; salt the cucumbers liberally. Leave for 15 to 30 minutes. Rinse and drain the cucumber slices. Squeeze water out of the cucumbers with hands or paper towels and move to a serving bowl.

Stir the sugar into the vinegar to dissolve, then pour over the sliced cucumbers. Sprinkle with green onions and sesame seeds.

Variation: Cooked Cucumber Crescent Salad

Add the seeded, sliced cucumbers to a pan and cook until crisp-tender, about 4 minutes. Add 2 tablespoons white vinegar, pinch salt and pepper, and stir in pinch of sugar. Cook until almost all the liquid has evaporated. Remove from the heat. Cool slightly and stir in ½ cup sour cream, 2 chopped green onions or scallions, and 2 tablespoons chopped basil or thyme. Cover and chill at least 2 hours or up to 2 days. Top with sesame seeds just before serving.

EGGPLANT

Select eggplant that has smooth, firm, glossy skin in colors from inky black to purple, in shapes from globes to teardrops, and that feels heavy for its size. Eggplant that feels light for its size is often spongy. Store eggplant wrapped in a paper towel and covered loosely with plastic. Use within 2 days to prevent bitterness from setting in.

Whether using a sharp kitchen peeler or knife, peeling the dark skin off of an eggplant is a nuisance. I peel only when I feel it is absolutely necessary, rarely for a family dish.

STUFFED EGG-PLANTS A LA CREOLE

"Parboil the egg-plants; cut them in halves; scoop out the inside, being careful not to break the outside skin, which you refill later with the following stuffing: Mix up the inside of the egg-plant with a slice of boiled ham chopped very fine, breadcrumbs, butter, salt, and pepper—shrimps if you have them, make a delicious addition; bind this stuffing with the yolk of an egg and fill your egg-plant skins; sprinkle with powdered breadcrumbs, put a small lump of butter on each piece, and bake."

—Mrs. Washington, *The Unrivalled Cook-Book and Housekeeper's Guide*, 1886

Chunky Eggplant Spread

MAKES 6 CUPS

Eggplant loves the Southern climate and soil; thus we have an abundance all summer long. It is difficult to brown if not degorged prior to cooking, as the eggplant contains water. If brownness is not essential, proceed as desired.

1 large eggplant

1/2 cup oil, divided

1 large onion, chopped

1/2 cup diced celery

2 cups or 1 (15-ounce) can peeled whole tomatoes, coarsely chopped

1–2 tablespoons tomato paste, optional

2 tablespoons red wine vinegar

1/3 cup pitted and sliced black olives

Salt

Freshly ground black pepper

2 tablespoons roasted peanuts

1/2 cup raisins

Crackers

Cut the eggplant into 1/2-inch cubes and degorge, if desired, for browning. Heat 1/4 cup oil in a heavy skillet. Add eggplant and cook in batches, not overcrowding the pan. Stir while cooking and browning; drain on paper towels. Add more oil to the pan as needed.

Add the onion and celery to the oil and cook 5 minutes, or until soft. Return the eggplant to the skillet. Add tomatoes, tomato paste, vinegar, and olives. Season to taste with salt and pepper. Simmer for 30 minutes, stirring occasionally.

Refrigerate, covered, for 30 minutes or up to several days, or freeze in an airtight container. Remove (and defrost if necessary) to a serving dish and top with peanuts and raisins.

Serve with crackers.

DEGORGING

Dégorger is a French cooking term meaning to use salt to draw water out of a food, such as eggplant or a cucumber. This is commonly done by sprinkling the sliced vegetable with salt and letting it sit in a colander for a period of time. After that, the vegetable is dried with a paper towel or rinsed in cold water and then dried. In this book, we use the English term *degorge*.

Eggplant and
Red Pepper Stew
(Southern Ratatouille)

Eggplant and Red Pepper Stew (Southern Ratatouille)

SERVES 10 TO 12

No two stews are the same, so don't feel constrained to duplicate this lush Southern version. With luck, all the vegetables are available at one time. Take the amount of vegetables on hand and adjust accordingly. For example, omit the tomatoes to make a zucchini, eggplant, and pepper casserole. Cut the recipe in half or double it. Just don't try to make it exact. "Go with the flow," as they say. And peeling of vegetables removes many good vitamins, so leave them unpeeled when possible.

4 large eggplants or 6 small ones

Salt

3 red, yellow, or green bell peppers

6 medium zucchini

6 medium onions

8 tablespoons oil, divided

6 garlic cloves, chopped

2 (14-ounce) cans Italian plum tomatoes with juice or 2 pounds fresh tomatoes, chopped

1 cup chopped fresh herbs: preferably thyme, parsley, and basil

Freshly ground black pepper

Preheat oven to 350 degrees.

Slice the eggplant lengthwise into ¼-inch-thick slices. Lightly score the flesh of the slices in a crosshatch pattern (like tic-tac-toe). Move the slices to a colander over a bowl or sink. Degorge (page 91) the eggplant for 30 minutes.

Meanwhile, seed the peppers, and then slice the zucchini, onions, and peppers. Discard the extracted liquid from the eggplant. Rinse, drain, and dry the eggplant well with paper towels. Brush the eggplant and zucchini slices with oil and move to an oiled rimmed baking sheet. Cook in the oven until lightly browned, about 20 minutes, turning halfway through.

Heat 2 tablespoons of the oil in a heavy-bottomed pan. Add the onions, peppers, and garlic, and cook about 30 minutes, until soft, adding oil as needed. Add the cooked eggplant, zucchini, tomatoes and their juices, and the herbs. Season well to taste with pepper. Serve hot or cold. Freezes well and easily reheats in the microwave.

Variation: Add two cups fresh lady peas. Continue to cook the ratatouille for another 1 hour, or until thick and creamy. It is savory and makes a wonderful bed for grilled pork or lamb chops or chicken breasts.

No-Fail Eggplant Lasagna

SERVES 6

Eggplant lasagna—where the eggplant substitutes for pasta—is extraordinarily welcome towards the end of July, when Southern garden vines tumble about together, their vegetables a bit oversized but still abundant, and the cook is looking for all-in-one dishes to beat the heat. Ideally, this recipe is doubled so that one portion is frozen for a fall evening. It likes being made ahead a few days, too, refrigerated until needed so the flavors meld. Eggplant in a dish like this has become regarded as a satisfying substitute for meat.

4–6 tablespoons oil

3 teaspoons finely chopped fresh basil, oregano, marjoram, and/or thyme

Salt

Freshly ground black pepper

1 large eggplant, sliced 1/2 inch thick

1 large zucchini, sliced 1/2 inch thick

1 cup freshly grated Parmesan cheese

1 cup ricotta cheese, drained

2 cups store-bought marinara sauce

2 tablespoons fennel seed, crushed or ground

8 ounces grated mozzarella cheese

Stir the oil with the herbs, salt, and pepper. Brush it onto both sides of the eggplant and zucchini. Lay the eggplant and zucchini in single layers on separate rimmed baking sheets, or move to a grill, using a grill basket if needed. Broil or grill 2 inches from the heat for 4 to 5 minutes, until light brown. Turn, brush the other side with the herbed oil, and broil until lightly browned and soft. Remove from broiler or grill.

Preheat oven to 350 degrees. Layer half of the eggplant slices in a wide, shallow 2- or 3-quart baking dish. Top with half of the zucchini. Layer in 1/2 cup Parmesan, 1/2 cup ricotta, 1 cup marinara sauce, and 1 tablespoon fennel seed. Repeat the layers with the remaining ingredients, finishing with the mozzarella. Cover and bake 20 to 25 minutes, until hot and bubbly.

This dish freezes well. To reheat, cover and defrost in the refrigerator before baking in a 350-degree oven for about 30 to 40 minutes, until heated through.

Variation: Blanch, sauté, and drain turnip greens, preferably small but cutting as necessary, and substitute for the zucchini.

GARLIC

Purchase firm, heavy bulbs and store in a well-ventilated space. Do not refrigerate. Garlic keeps for up to a month, but toss any that are soft or mildewed.

Preparing and measuring—Smash a garlic clove in its skin to pop out the clove. Chop the garlic clove finely, discarding the tough end piece. Measure with a measuring spoon. Move to the hollow of a cupped hand. This is one garlic clove, chopped. Try to use the hollow of a hand to measure salt, garlic, and other regular condiments, to save time in measuring.

To separate the garlic cloves, lay a knife horizontally across the top of the garlic head and smash the knife down on the head, breaking apart the cloves. To peel an individual clove, lay a knife flat on top of the clove and swack it.

Making garlic paste—Sprinkle a wooden board with salt; add peeled garlic cloves, and scrape the garlic and salt together with the end of a small knife. The salt's abrasiveness will turn the garlic into a paste. This paste can be made in advance and kept wrapped in the refrigerator.

Cooking garlic—When cooked whole, garlic cloves are sweet and become smooth and spreadable. There are two ways to achieve this. One is to cook the whole head; another is to cook the cloves only. Whole garlic may be cooked in the microwave. The cloves tend to pop open and splatter, so cook, covered, and on medium power for 1 minute; check and cook a bit more if necessary. Garlic cloves also soften when boiled, sautéed, or baked.

Alternatively, remove only the papery exterior from whole garlic, rub with oil, wrap with foil or place in another ovenproof container, and roast at 350 degrees for approximately 1 hour, depending on size; check after 30 minutes. Garlic also takes to being boiled in water or stock.

GREEN GARLIC

Immature garlic bulbs have several stages, including using the early stalk. The small bulbs covered with a filmy white skin are called "garlic in a chemise" by the French.

GREENS

Greens are beloved by Southerners, feeding them in hard times and good. The origins of their popularity come from African as well as European cooks. An important source of calcium and other nutrients, greens enjoy flavor enhancement and gain protein from the addition of "seasoning" meat. Seasoning meat includes rinsed and sliced salt pork, ham hock, streak o' lean, other pieces of cured pork (page 99), and other smoked meats.

The most popular types of greens in the South are collard and turnip greens, and it is these that are generally meant when "greens" are referred to. There are numerous varieties of turnip tops and turnip greens. When cooking its tops, the turnip is frequently added to the greens. Turnip greens are preferred by those who like to add other vegetables, such as potatoes, to a cooking liquid.

Collards grow as cabbage-like leaves but they have no root vegetable. They do have a pungent odor when cooked. Their stalk is tough and is removed before cooking. Smaller varieties are now being grown that have less odor.

I never thought of kale as a Southern vegetable until my husband said he grew up with it. The many new varieties have made it fashionable roasted, in salads, and as a side. Chard is a recent addition to the table. Rainbow chard, with its bright red stems, has a sharp spinach-like flavor. Remove the stems and set aside. Tear the greens as with any other green, and steam, sauté, or roast the stems as with asparagus.

Poke sallet is a wild indigenous green that can grow six feet tall but is usually eaten like turnip greens when it is a smaller plant and has a mild taste. Like other greens, it becomes bitter and tough as it ages. Small stems of poke sallet can be cooked much like asparagus, but its roots and berries are inedible. It is called poke sallet, or poke, allegedly because it was put into a sack, or poke, when picked.

Other greens include cabbage, sorrel, rape, dock, beet and broccoli greens, and lambs quarters. Cressi (also spelled *cresse*) grows wild near the banks of streams and is much like watercress.

Purchasing greens and storing—Buy greens that are crisp and have a bright green color. Avoid wilted or yellowing greens. Store unwashed greens in the refrigerator for up to 3 or 4 days. One and a half pounds of fresh leaves yields one cup of cooked and drained leaves.

Washing greens—Prewashed greens are widely available, but care should still be taken to be sure they are free of dirt; it can take up to two or three washings to get them clean. Collard greens still on the stalk are sturdy enough to be held under running water, turned, and washed on the second side. Continue going through the leaves until all are well rinsed.

For other greens, remove leaves from stalks, discarding any tough greens and stalks (tender stalks may be tossed with oil and roasted). Fill a basin with cold salted water, add the loose greens, stir several times in the water, and soak. Remove the greens from the basin before tipping off the water, making sure not to pour dirt back over the greens still in the basin. Rub the greens and see if any grit is left on the leaves. If so, rinse again.

De-stemming and preparing greens—Fold the large leaves lengthwise at the stem. Pull the tough portion of the stem away from the leaf starting where the leaf meets the stem at the bottom, and discard the stem. The stem may also be cut away with a knife. Stack several de-stemmed leaves together and roll. Use a sharp knife to cut down the roll in 1-inch pieces.

Many Southern homes used to keep a bottle of vinegar infused with peppers on the kitchen table (the closer to Louisiana, the hotter the concoction). Greens were sprinkled with vinegar or hot sauce before eating. Sriracha and other hot sauces are now raising the heat. Cynthia's grandmother made her own pepper vinegar with Datil peppers.

A Mess of Greens and "Pot Likker"

SERVES 6 TO 8, INCLUDING "POT LIKKER"

A "mess" of greens, as cooked greens are called, is an armful of bundles of turnips or collards that cook down to a quart of greens in addition to the broth. Regarded as a comfort food, greens can be a meal, eaten just by themselves or with cornbread or biscuits, as well as part of a larger meal. When meat was a rarity, the seasoning meat in greens was an important dietary supplement, with the fat giving energy for long days and cold nights. Greens are best when picked after the first frost, customarily around hog-butchering time, when there is a snap in the air, or in early spring; but there is hardly a time anymore when they are not available.

1/3 pound sliced, rinsed salt pork or streak o' lean, smoked neck, or other cured pork

1–2 slices onion, optional

1 small hot pepper, optional

5 pounds turnip, collard, poke sallet, or kale greens, washed (page 97)

Salt

Freshly ground pepper

Hot sauce, optional

Bring 1/2 gallon of water to the boil; add the pork, optional onion, and hot pepper and return to the boil. If time is available, cook about 30 minutes to flavor the broth.

Meanwhile, tear off and discard from the greens the stalks and any tough veins. Tear or cut the remaining greens into pieces and add to the broth. Return to the boil, reduce the heat to a simmer, pushing any bobbing greens down into the liquid, and cover. Cook 50 minutes to 3 hours, as desired. Take a pair of large scissors and cut any pieces larger than bite-size. Taste and season with salt, pepper, and hot sauce as desired. Serve with the broth (pot likker), or strain, reserving the broth for another time. Cooked greens will last covered and refrigerated for several days. They freeze up to 3 months.

Variations:

• When the greens have returned to the boil, add peeled and cut-up turnips or beets, and cook until the vegetables are done, about half an hour, depending on size.

• Add small pieces of potatoes to the boiling greens and cook until the potatoes are done, about 30 minutes, depending on size.

• Before serving, break up pieces of cornbread and add to bowls of pot likker as desired.

SEASONING MEATS FOR VEGETABLES

There is a long tradition of seasoning cooked vegetables with the broth of pork and other bones and meats. While outsiders may find these vegetables greasy, to Southerners accustomed to them, they are full of flavor and richness. They may be eaten at a meal where no other meat is provided, which is probably the origin in an era when meat was a treat on Sunday, if then. Less fortunate people, including slaves, had only the less desirable parts of the pig for their meals and seasonings. The best known of these many parts are fatback, streak o' lean, and hog jowl. Any overly salted meat should be rinsed.

Fatback—(Also called salt pork.) This comes from the back of the pig and can be salted, smoked, or, in some cases, left fresh. Primarily fat, it is frequently sold sliced, with just a slice going into the pan with the water and vegetables. It may also be sautéed and eaten as a side meat.

Streak o' lean—This comes from the belly of the pork and is sold salted, smoked, or in some cases left fresh. It is fattier than bacon but also may be sautéed and eaten as a side meat. The pronunciation is run together: "streakolean."

Pork belly—For those of us used to pork belly as a seasoning meat, it is now a fearful time, as this once inexpensive piece of meat is becoming popular—fresh, sautéed, or broiled. A cured piece is sometimes called "white bacon"; it is flavorsome soaked in water and then thinly sliced, fried, and served with cream gravy.

Hog jowl—A portion or the whole hog jowl (cheek), usually just the bone and what clings to it, is a favorite for seasoning black-eyed peas and turnip greens for New Year's Day and other holidays.

In addition to any part of cured ham, meats used for seasoning also include split pig tails, feet, hocks, and other pig parts—whether smoked, salted, or fresh. Smoked turkey necks and other smoked meats and poultry are also used as seasoning meats.

CHIFFONADE

To chiffonade is to roll into several layers and cut into very thin strips, as with greens or basil. Stack washed and deveined greens. Roll into a cigar shape. Lay flat on the board and slice horizontally ¼ inch thick, or thinner for herbs.

Sautéed Chiffonade of Turnip, Collard, Kale, or Baby Beet Greens with Beets

SERVES 4 TO 6

New, less bitter varieties of greens developed in the last twenty years, as well as recent use of smaller and younger greens, have led to exciting, dashing dishes like this. Beet, plain or red kale, turnip or collard greens all work singly or together. If very large or tough greens are all that is available, blanch in boiling water for 1 to 2 minutes, drain, and proceed.

1 pound greens, washed (page 97)

2 teaspoons butter or oil

2 garlic cloves, chopped

1 teaspoon finely chopped fresh ginger

1 pound cooked beets or 1 (8-ounce) can beets, drained and coarsely chopped

2 tablespoons freshly squeezed lemon juice or cider vinegar

Salt

Freshly ground black pepper

Remove stems of greens if necessary and chiffonade the greens. Melt the butter in a large skillet and add the chiffonaded greens, garlic, and ginger. Cover and cook until the greens are wilted, just a few minutes. Stir in the chopped beets and lemon juice. Season to taste with salt and pepper. Heat through for 1 to 2 minutes and serve hot or at room temperature.

Sautéed Chiffonade
of Turnip, Collard,
Kale, or Baby Beet
Greens with Beets

Fried Greens

SERVES 4

I served these greens, which are easily made ahead of time, as garnishes in my restaurant in Social Circle, Georgia. Although Cynthia's husband says we will fry anything in the South, these are deservedly exceptional. Be sure to dry the greens thoroughly or their moisture will cause the oil to bubble over.

1 pound turnip or collard greens, washed

Shortening or vegetable oil for frying

Salt, optional

Freshly ground black pepper, optional

Ground hot red pepper, optional

Stem the greens and remove the veins. Chiffonade (page 100) the greens into $1/8$-inch-wide ribbons. Spread out on paper towel-lined baking sheets to dry for at least 10 minutes, or a few hours if necessary. Dry very well with paper towels. Pour enough oil to reach the halfway mark into a heavy skillet or deep-fat fryer, and heat to 350 degrees. When hot, cover hands with a mitt or kitchen towel and add the dry greens by the handful—the fat will boil up considerably. Fry until crisp, about 1–2 minutes. Remove all the greens with a Chinese-type or slotted strainer and drain on a paper towel. Continue to fry in batches until all the greens are cooked. They will last several hours unsalted (salt causes them to wilt). Just before serving, season to taste with salt, pepper, and hot red pepper if using.

Simple Sautéed Greens

SERVES 4 TO 6

All greens can be cooked this way when tender. Avoid large greens for this recipe. My beloved Celeste Dupree, my favorite former mother-in-law, grew turnip greens in her annual garden. She would eat the tender baby ones in a salad or cook them as a quick sauté.

2 pounds small greens, washed (page 97)	Salt
2–4 tablespoons butter	Freshly ground black pepper

Remove any tough veins, stalks, or stems from the greens. Melt the butter in a large frying pan. Toss the still-damp greens in the butter until well coated. (If dry, add $1/3$ cup water). Cover the pan and cook 3 to 5 minutes, until wilted. Season to taste with salt and pepper.

Variations:

• Add 1 cup heavy cream to the pan after removing the greens, bring to the boil, and let boil down to about $2/3$ cup.

• Cook the butter until it turns a nutty brown before adding the greens.

• Substitute oil for the butter and add chopped garlic to the pan.

• Substitute frozen spinach, collards, or kale, defrosted and well drained.

• Top sautéed mushrooms, onions, garlic, and/or tomatoes with the still-damp greens before covering and wilting.

Julia's Kale Chips

Once you try these baked kale chips, you'll wonder why you waste your time snacking on any other chip.

1 bunch kale, washed and stems removed

1 teaspoon salt

½ teaspoon freshly ground black pepper

1 tablespoon oil

Preheat oven to 400 degrees.

Tear the kale into bite-size pieces and toss with the salt, pepper, and oil. Depending on quantity, spread out in a single layer on one or two rimmed baking sheets.

Bake approximately 10 minutes. Keep a close watch to see that the pieces have crisped without browning too much. If the kale has been layered on the baking sheet too much, it will take an extra minute or two.

When the chips are finished, remove from the oven and serve immediately. These do not keep well, so enjoy them in one sitting.

Variation: Toss stems or small stalks in oil and bake as above for a cook's treat.

Layered Oven-Roasted Mixed Vegetables

SERVES 4 TO 6

Our friend Jennet Alterman, a treasure to Charleston, makes this heartwarming winter dish.

1 pound turnip greens, washed (page 97)

2 medium onions, sliced

2 large tomatoes, sliced

Salt

Freshly ground black pepper

Chopped fresh thyme, rosemary, or basil

3 tablespoons oil

Tear off and discard from the greens the stalks and any tough veins. Tear or cut the remaining greens. Coat a casserole dish with 1 tablespoon oil and alternate layers turnip greens, a few sliced onions, and sliced tomatoes, sprinkling with salt and pepper to taste, drizzling with oil between layers and on top. Sprinkle with optional herbs. Cover tightly with foil and bake 20 minutes. Remove foil and bake 10 minutes. Serve hot.

Variations:

• Add quartered or halved baby potatoes or sliced broccoli stems.

• Add grated cheese to the layers.

Collard, Turnip Greens, or Kale Salad

SERVES 2

Collards and turnip greens have varied lives. My favorite former husband's stepmother ate both in salads in the spring and the late fall, when the greens were small and tender. She even eschewed any dressing and just ate them plain. As time goes on, they have a brief window when they can be rolled up like a cigar and shredded and added to other salads, as we do with arugula. They can also be substituted for dandelion and other bitter greens. Then they pass into the bitter vegetable stage and need to be blanched, sautéed, or long cooked. By all means, try the variations, as they put the salad over the top!

1 cup baby collard, turnip greens, or kale, washed (page 97)

½ cup Basic Vinaigrette (page 196)

Salt

Freshly ground black pepper

Remove any stems from the greens and toss the washed, dried greens with enough vinaigrette to coat lightly. Season to taste with salt and pepper.

Variations:

• Add ¼ to ⅓ cup crumbled goat, cream or Boursin cheese.

• Add ¼ to ⅓ cup slivered country ham.

• Add ¼ cup fresh herbs such as basil, lemon thyme, or marjoram.

• Rub the greens gently all over with olive oil to make a tender, limper green.

SALAD GREENS AND LETTUCES

From tender baby lettuces to sturdy head lettuces, the greens of a salad are as varied as an artist's palette. Iceberg was once the most common green salad served, particularly in restaurants, but it has thankfully been displaced by Boston, Bibb, escarole, frisée, kale, mâche, romaine, radicchio, red leaf, and others. By far the best-tasting lettuces are those picked fresh from the garden or purchased from the local farmers market. Plastic boxes and bags of salad mixes are popular items in the produce section but must be eyed carefully for rotting leaves before purchasing and used within a couple of days once purchased. Mesclun mix is a popular mix of little wild greens and lettuces, but as there is no standard for what it contains, we much prefer combining our own.

Arugula is a new green to the South, and it thrives in our soil and heat. In England it is called rocket, and in Italy it is rucola. It can be eaten alone, mixed with other greens, or used as a bed or topping for ingredients from fish to other vegetables.

Washing salad greens—Salad greens are delicate, so they should be added to a large bowl or pan of cold water rather than being run under the faucet, where they will crack, creating teeny holes that make the salad soggy after the vinaigrette is added. After gently stirring the greens in the cold water, let them rest. Pick them up and put into a colander. There will be dirt and sand in the bottom of the bowl, so avoid dumping the whole shebang into a colander and adding the dirt back in! Usually the greens will have to be rinsed the same way a second time. Check for grit—there is nothing worse—and if necessary, repeat a third time. Salad spinners work well as long as the fragile greens are not whirred in a sudden frenzy. We

usually pat them dry in a tea towel, wrap, and refrigerate. In the restaurant I would layer them in the tea towels in the refrigerator crisper. Shirley Corriher shared a marvelous trick of putting them into a plastic bag and sucking out the excess air with a straw. This helps them last much longer.

Building a salad—Salad greens are only the beginning to a great salad. Fresh herbs, vegetables, fruit, and nuts all add color, texture, and taste to a salad. Delicate herbs such as basil, parsley, and tarragon mix well in a salad, whereas woody herbs like rosemary are less pleasing due to their texture. Fresh or cooked vegetables add crunch and color. Fresh fruit (even grilled or caramelized) brings a touch of sweetness, and nuts (raw or roasted) add more crunch.

When preparing the salad greens, tear (do not cut) the leaves into pieces large enough to pierce with a fork, but not too small, as smaller pieces absorb too much dressing and wilt quickly. Cutting the leaves with a knife or scissors bruises the leaves. Count on about two handfuls of greens per person for a starter salad or one that is served with a meal. A meal salad would increase to three or so handfuls per person.

Dressing a Salad—Dress a green salad just before serving, to prevent the leaves from wilting and browning from acid in the vinaigrette. Add the salad to a large, wide bowl and drizzle dressing on top. Toss to coat the leaves lightly in dressing. Add more dressing as needed. Remove individual portions to individual serving plates after tossing, to keep the leaves from getting soggy from sitting in the extra dressing.

MUSHROOMS

Whether eaten by themselves, on top of a steak or fish, or tossed over pasta, rice, or vegetables, mushrooms are a handy part of our cuisine. Many kinds of wild mushrooms grow naturally in the South, although only experts know where to find them anymore. From South Carolina to Virginia, morel, chanterelle, and shiitake hunters closely guard their secret places. Only the trained should search for and eat wild mushrooms. For the rest of us, cultivated must do. Cultivated mushrooms have been grown sporadically in the South since at least the 1970s, perhaps even earlier.

Dried mushrooms are a convenient resource. Inspect before purchase to avoid a package of all stems and pieces. Soak in boiling liquid, which itself becomes flavorful. The broth should always be strained before using in soups, stocks, sauces, or grain dishes.

Purchasing mushrooms—Buy mushrooms that are dry and firm. Avoid any that are slimy. Wrap mushrooms loosely in paper towels and refrigerate for two or three days.

Preparing mushrooms—After years of saying otherwise, authorities now say that washing and soaking mushrooms does not cause them to absorb more water. But I still prefer brushing or wiping them clean: use a damp paper towel that has been dipped in salt, or a mushroom brush, to brush away any dirt. Another way to clean without soaking is to spray them rapidly with a sink water sprayer. Mushrooms are harder to chop when soggy.

Slice off the end of the stems if tough or wizened. They have nutrition and flavor, so save them to flavor broth.

Sautéed Mushrooms

SERVES 2 TO 4

Simple sautéed mushrooms can be eaten alone or added to most any dish, whether fresh or reconstituted (see below). They add variation and flavor and are now easy to have on hand.

1/2–1 pound fresh or reconstituted mushrooms, cleaned

2 tablespoons butter

Salt

Freshly ground black pepper

Remove any brown or tough stems and put them aside for another purpose. Slice the mushrooms if large, or leave whole if small. Heat the butter in a frying pan. Add the mushrooms and sauté about 3 to 5 minutes, until tender but cooked. Season to taste with salt and pepper. Serve hot. May be refrigerated or frozen and reheated.

Variations:

• Sauté 2 chopped garlic cloves, 1 chopped shallot or small onion, and chopped fresh herbs or ginger. Add mushrooms and cook as above.

• Ideal to perk up leftovers, sautéed mushrooms can enhance egg dishes, scrambled eggs, frittatas, cooked asparagus, broccoli florets or stalks, butter beans, carrots, zucchini, green beans, snow peas, and more. Cook mushrooms separately, then combine and reheat with the vegetable of your choice and top with a tablespoon of sesame seeds.

• In themselves or added to sauces, they provide a sophisticated boost for steak, chops, chicken breasts, and more.

Indispensable Mushrooms with Greens

Indispensable Mushrooms with Greens

SERVES 16

Party food should be pretty, easy to assemble, easy to serve, as well as delicious. Button mushrooms fit the bill perfectly. They can be made ahead and reheated easily and filled with anything from beef stew to foie gras. These button mushrooms can be eaten with one bite, but please do serve with napkins if not a plate. Large mushrooms will need a plate and should be served at a sit-down meal. Any leftover filling can be added to rice, couscous, or a Sunday omelet, or frozen.

¾ pound fresh spinach or baby turnip greens, washed (page 97)

2 pounds small mushrooms, cleaned

1 cup butter, divided

2 medium onions, chopped

3 garlic cloves, chopped

½ cup fine breadcrumbs, or panko

½ teaspoon Dijon mustard

Salt

Freshly ground black pepper

½ cup grated Parmesan cheese

Preheat oven to 350 degrees.

Remove and discard any stems and tough leaves from the greens. Chop the leaves in a food processor. If greens are large, blanch briefly and drain well. Remove and chop the stems of the mushrooms and set aside.

Melt ½ cup butter in a Dutch oven or deep skillet over medium heat, and dip the mushroom caps into it until well coated on all sides. Place them top side down on a greased rimmed baking sheet.

Heat remaining butter in the skillet; add the onions, garlic, and chopped mushroom stems, and sauté until very soft, about 10 minutes. Add the greens and cook a few minutes until wilted; drain off and reserve some of the liquid. Add the breadcrumbs and mustard, and mix well. Add back some of the reserved liquid if the mixture is so dry that it doesn't stick together easily. This filling can be made several days in advance or frozen and defrosted before stuffing mushrooms. Season to taste with salt and pepper.

Fill each buttered mushroom cap (up to 1 day in advance) with this mixture, mounding it high, and sprinkle with Parmesan cheese. Bake 10 to 15 minutes. Any leftovers freeze fine for the family, but not for company, as they get brown and weepy.

Variation: Add ½ cup finely chopped ham, crisp bacon, sautéed sausage, chopped shrimp, crabmeat, or smoked turkey. Garnish with chopped herbs or small whole shrimp.

Grilled Portobello Mushroom Steaks

SERVES 4 TO 6

Portobello mushrooms (a larger variety of the cremini mushrooms) are now grown all over the United States, including the South. They may be treated like a steak—served whole or sliced and added to another dish.

4–6 medium-sized portobello mushrooms, each about 4 inches across

Salt

6 garlic cloves, finely chopped

4–6 tablespoons olive oil

Freshly ground black pepper

Fresh herbs, optional

Clean the mushrooms; remove the stems and reserve them for another use. Shake the salt, garlic, olive oil, and pepper in a plastic bag. Add the mushrooms, seal the bag, and turn to coat the mushrooms in the oil. Marinate up to 1 hour.

Grill top side up for 4 to 5 minutes, or broil the mushrooms on a broiler pan. Flip the mushrooms and cook 4 more minutes. The mushrooms should be well cooked on the outside but creamy and tender on the inside. Sprinkle with fresh herbs if using. Serve whole or sliced.

Variations:

• Serve in a crusty burger bun with Cheddar cheese, lettuce, ripe tomato, and a slice of red onion.

OKRA

Okra, a flowering plant like its cousins cotton, cocoa, and hibiscus, loves poor soil, unpredictable rains, and heat. It does not like frost, which is why many living above the Mason-Dixon Line are unfamiliar with its goodness or view it with suspicion—odd, since so much of the world relishes it. In India it is called "lady fingers," its graceful pods curving into a slender tip much like a lady's finger. Africans frequently call it "gumbo," a term that has taken root in Louisiana and other Cajun areas as well as in the Gullah region of South Carolina and Georgia.

Okra's origins are iffy. The earliest report of it was in the 1200s by a Spaniard visiting Egypt, where it had most likely originated from Ethiopia. It spread to the Americas in the mid-1600s, with Thomas Jefferson viewing it as commonplace by the late-eighteenth century. Most likely it came to the South by way of slave traders. It is improbable that Africans themselves brought it over, regardless of the apocrypha about poking seeds in their ears or hair arrangements.

The worst thing about okra is picking it—its fibrous exterior has a fuzziness that clings and can cause itching, and the plant is aggressive in the way it protects the flowers from which the okra emerges. Both the flower and the okra are edible, as are the leaves. The flower

is stuffed or fried; the leaves are cooked like beets or other greens.

Okra's multiple seeds are reluctant to leave the pentagon in which they are nestled—it's rare for an okra seed to spill out, even when stir-frying. Stir-frying, frying, roasting, and grilling deter the mucilaginous quality inherent in okra. So, too, does acid, which is why it is so frequently paired with tomatoes or citrus, or put up as a pickle. It has a crisp texture when eaten raw, and its mild flavor is well suited to cooking alone or with other vegetables.

Buying and storing okra—When buying okra, look for the smallest pods. By the time larger pods are cooked, they are much less palatable. If the smaller ones are not available, slice the larger ones on the diagonal before preparing.

To freeze okra, spread it out separately on a flat surface during an initial freeze, then collect and keep in a freezer container. It is sold fresh, frozen, and canned. Canned okra is pressure-cooked, so it has a pronounced mucilaginous quality.

Stir-Fried Okra

SERVES 2 TO 3

Simply cooked okra is welcome in the middle of the hot summer, when heating up the kitchen is undesirable.

2–4 tablespoons butter

1 pound okra, sliced diagonally, caps discarded

Salt

Freshly ground black pepper

Heat the butter in a large skillet. Add the sliced okra and sauté 3 to 4 minutes, until crisp-tender. Season to taste with salt and pepper. Serve hot. May be reheated.

Variations:

• Sliver okra by removing the caps and thinly slicing the okra vertically for a completely different look. Continue as above in Stir-Fried Okra.

• Add to other sautéed vegetables, such as corn, mushrooms, or grape tomato halves.

Iron Skillet Okra

SERVES 6

The quantity of lightly coated crisp okra in this recipe may seem excessive for the number of people, but experience has taught me that it has a popcorn quality, inviting nibblers by its aroma and texture, and the first batch will be eaten before the second is done. If crisp enough, it can be reheated in a 350-degree oven, but watch carefully to prevent burning. Smaller okra may not need slicing, but remove the tough caps. (Pre-battered frozen okra sold commercially is inferior.) As a friend of mine said, stirring fried and delicate foods is a temptation of the devil. Stirring okra while it fries accomplishes nothing except knocking off the coating, which causes it to burn easily. Turn the okra if necessary (the okra should turn itself when brown, but use a slotted spoon to turn it if necessary). Practice "benign neglect." Removing it should be the only time it is disturbed.

2 pounds okra	Shortening or vegetable oil for frying
¾ cup cornmeal	Salt
¾ cup all-purpose flour	Freshly ground black pepper
3 teaspoons salt	

Line a rimmed baking sheet with paper towels. Wash and lightly drain okra in a colander so it will retain enough moisture for the flour mixture to adhere. Cut off and discard caps, and slice okra into $1/2$-inch slices or pieces. Toss together the cornmeal, flour, and salt, and toss with a portion of the okra. Remove the okra and spread on waxed paper to dry for a few minutes. Toss again in cornmeal mixture to coat thoroughly, avoiding clumping. Repeat with remaining okra. The okra can be left up to several hours in the meal mixture to gather a thicker crust.

Meanwhile, pour enough oil into an iron skillet or deep frying pan to reach halfway up the side, and heat oil to 350 degrees. To be sure the oil is hot enough, add a test piece of okra. Bubbles should sizzle around the okra. Add the floured okra in batches, leaving enough room in the pan to turn the okra. Brown lightly on both sides. Resist the temptation to turn the okra too soon; give it a chance to turn itself. If stirred too much, the cornmeal will fall to the bottom of the pan and burn. When brown and crisp, remove okra to paper towels to drain. If necessary, carefully drain the oil into a metal bowl and wipe the bottom of the pan clean of browned bits. With pot holders, pour the drained oil back into the pan and repeat with the second batch. Season to taste with salt and pepper.

Variation: Omit the flour and just use cornmeal.

Roasted Okra Chips

MAKES 2 CUPS

Familiar to those raised in warm-weather or tropical climates, this pentagonal-shaped vegetable is harvested in the summertime from a hibiscus family tree that can grow 6 to 8 feet high. When asked to describe one characteristic of this vegetable, people will usually mention something about it being slimy, perhaps the main motivation when preparing these chips. The results were tiny crispy chips that became irresistible and blessedly "slime free."

20 okra (about 3 cups, sliced vertically or horizontally)

2 tablespoons oil

½ teaspoon salt

½ teaspoon pepper

Preheat oven to 350 degrees.

Toss sliced okra gently with oil, salt, and pepper in a large bowl. Move okra onto a rimmed baking sheet and roast for 10 to 15 minutes. Turn okra to the other side halfway through the cooking time. Total time to cook the okra depends on the thickness of the slice, so adjust baking time accordingly. Remove from oven when crispy and transfer to a paper towel. Any leftovers can be refrigerated. They will lose their crispiness but may be reheated.

Variation: Cynthia roasts her okra whole, following the method above, and keeps them on hand for snacking.

Variation: Grilled Okra

Slice okra or leave whole. Toss gently with oil, salt, and pepper in a large bowl. Preheat a grill pan on the stove, or preheat the grill to medium. Add the okra to the hot pan or grill and cook for 5 to 6 minutes per side. Remove when crispy.

One large okra yields about 8 to 10 slices, and a small one about 5 to 7 slices. Try slicing the okra from tip to tip on a diagonal to get a 2-inch-long slice.

Deep-Fried Okra

SERVES 6

This crisp, thick exterior was developed by Margaret Lupo, longtime owner of Mary Mac's Tea Room in Atlanta. She was a dear friend, independent, competent, a mixture of tender and tough herself. Neither Cynthia nor I have deep-fryers.

2 pounds okra, well rinsed

1 egg, beaten

2 tablespoons water

2 cups buttermilk

4 teaspoons salt, divided

2 cups all-purpose flour

2 cups crushed cracker meal or saltines, crushed to the consistency of cornmeal

Freshly ground black pepper

Shortening or vegetable oil for frying

Line a rimmed baking sheet with paper towels. Cut the stem ends off the cleaned okra and slice $\frac{1}{4}$ inch thick. Mix together the egg, water, buttermilk, and 2 teaspoons salt in a large bowl. Toss the okra in the mixture.

Mix the flour, cracker meal, remaining salt, and pepper in another bowl. Remove okra from the buttermilk with a slotted spoon and add by spoonfuls to the flour. Toss lightly to coat, then move to a cake rack to remove excess flour.

Meanwhile, heat the oil in an electric skillet, wok, or deep frying pan to 350 degrees. Add the okra by large spoonfuls and fry until golden brown, turning only as necessary. Move with a slotted spoon to the paper towels to drain. Keep warm in a 250-degree oven while frying the remaining okra. Serve hot.

COATING OKRA

The two methods mentioned here and on page 115 allow the coating to stay crisp, and the okra can be reheated or snacked on at room temperature. A lighter batter quickly wilts on fried okra.

Okra and Tomatoes

Some genius, long before The Virginia House-Wife *was written, realized that acid in tomatoes countered the mucilaginous quality of okra. With this discovery, okra and tomatoes became the basis of many vegetable dishes and soups. I prefer adding onions and garlic to my basic recipe. I usually make it with canned tomatoes, but my husband was brought up with fresh ones. His South Carolina family always served this dish over rice.*

3 tablespoons butter	2 cups okra, caps removed and sliced
1 small onion, chopped	Salt
1–2 garlic cloves, chopped	Freshly ground black pepper
2–3 cups canned diced tomatoes with juice	Granulated sugar, optional

Melt the butter in a heavy saucepan. Add the onion and cook until soft, about 3 to 5 minutes. Add the garlic and cook 1 minute more. Add the tomatoes and okra, and bring to the boil. Reduce heat to a simmer and cook uncovered until thick, about 45 minutes to 1 hour, stirring as needed. Season to taste with salt and pepper. If the tomatoes taste "tinny," add a little sugar to smooth out the flavor.

Variation: Fresh Tomatoes and Okra

Peel and seed 4 to 5 large tomatoes to substitute for the canned tomatoes.

Variation: Okra with Corn and Tomatoes

Scrape corn off the cob and add to the pot 5 minutes before serving.

Marinated Okra

These still-crunchy okra make for an unusual finger food. Leave the cap on or, if necessary, trim carefully, leaving a minimum of cap on. Unfortunately these lose their color and become gray.

1 pound okra, caps removed

1/4 cup red wine or sherry vinegar

1/2 cup olive oil

1 tablespoon Dijon mustard

Grated rind of 1 small orange, no white attached

3 tablespoons freshly squeezed orange juice

1–2 teaspoons ground cumin

Salt

Freshly ground black pepper

Add uncapped okra to a pan of boiling water for 30 seconds. Drain and run quickly under cold water to stop the cooking. Set aside to cool.

Whisk together the remaining ingredients. Pour over the okra in a bowl and cover; marinate several hours or overnight. Drain and arrange on a serving platter to be eaten as a finger food, or on individual salad plates.

Variation: Season with coriander or fennel seed, either whole or grated, as desired.

Okra Pilau

Okra Pilau

SERVES 4

This recipe from Two Hundred Years of Charleston Cooking *gives great credit to Sally Washington, an African-American woman who was "a genius in her own right or else Charleston was gifted by the Gods" and was Mrs. Rhett's cook. We have adapted it here.*

8 slices bacon, diced

1 cup okra, sliced into small pieces

1 cup rice

2 cups water

Brown the bacon in a heavy frying pan. Remove and set aside on paper towels to drain, reserving fat. Add okra to the hot fat over low heat. Add the rice and water; cover and let cook until done, about 40 minutes. Remove from heat, toss in a bowl, top with the bacon dice, and serve.

Variation: Okra Pilau II

Add 1 copped onion and 1 tablespoon chopped green bell pepper to the bacon fat and sauté until light brown. Add 2 cups stewed tomatoes and 2 cups thinly sliced okra to the hot pan. Cook over medium heat until the tomatoes are reduced, about 15 minutes. Add 2 cups cooked rice and 1 teaspoon of salt; turn into the top of a double boiler or rice steamer, and let steam for 15 to 20 minutes. Top with crumbled bacon just before serving. Serves 6.

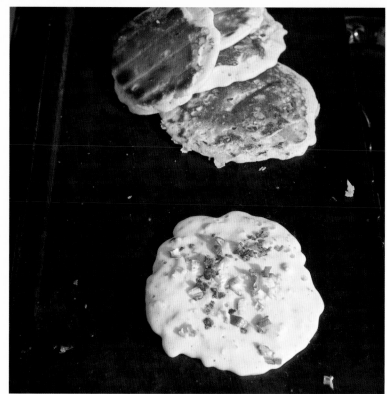

Okra Griddle Cakes

Okra Griddle Cakes

MAKES 16 CAKES

Flavors dance in the mouth in these batter cakes. This is an ideal starter for when guests' arrival time is uncertain, or when a kitchen gathering is the order of the day. Have everything ready ahead of time except the cakes. These are just enough to whet the appetite, a cross between fried okra and cornbread.

1½ cups self-rising cornmeal mix, see sidebar

½ cup all-purpose flour

1 tablespoon granulated sugar

2 cups buttermilk

3 tablespoons butter, melted

2 large eggs, lightly beaten

4 slices cooked bacon, finely chopped, drippings reserved

1 cup cooked okra, finely chopped

Shortening or vegetable oil for frying

Sour cream, optional

Up to 2 hours before serving, whisk together cornmeal mix, flour, and sugar in a bowl. Stir in buttermilk, butter, and eggs until just mixed. Add finely chopped bacon and okra to batter.

Heat a griddle or large iron skillet until hot. Add enough oil to coat the bottom. Sprinkle in a bit of batter to test that the pan is hot enough to sizzle and that the batter is a pourable consistency. Add water to thin if necessary, 2 tablespoons at a time. Ladle ¼ cup batter for each griddle cake onto hot griddle and cook until the top of the pancake is dotted with large bubbles and the bottom is light brown. Turn with a large spatula, and cook until the other side is lightly browned. Keep warm in a 200-degree oven on a rack over a baking sheet or serve immediately. Continue with the rest of the batter until all is gone. Serve hot with optional sour cream.

Variations:

• Top the sour cream with a little chopped bacon and okra.

• Substitute a little chopped turnip greens and hot pepper, a few chopped shrimp, or crab in the batter for the okra and bacon.

GRIDDLE CAKES

Griddle cakes can be made thick or thin, coin- or pancake-sized. What's necessary is a hot pan—and a watchful eye. The batter must be hot enough to rise in bubbles to the top of the pancake, indicating it is ready to turn, or a goopy mess will result. Use a ¼-cup ladle or measuring cup to make pouring easier.

To make self-rising cornmeal mix, combine 1½ cups cornmeal, 3 tablespoons flour, 1 tablespoon baking powder, and ½ teaspoon salt.

Okra Salad

Okra Salad

SERVES 4

This cool salad from the raw okra is refreshing and a welcome relief from cooking in the summer. If, however, you would like to stir-fry this briefly, it would be equally welcome.

½ pound okra

2 tablespoons olive oil

1 tablespoon grated lemon or orange rind, no white attached

Salt

Barely trim the cap end of the okra. Slice okra thinly on the diagonal. Toss with olive oil. Sprinkle with lemon. Salt if desired.

Variations:

• Add cooked shrimp.

• Toss with grated Parmesan, salt, and freshly ground pepper.

ONIONS, LEEKS, AND SHALLOTS

There are an endless variety of uses for the onion—from freshly chopped white ones in cucumber salad, to deeply caramelized ones for tarts, soups, and steaks, not to mention crispy fried ones for a side dish. Each way they taste a little different, bringing something else to the table.

Onions are the most forgiving of friends in the kitchen. They rarely need to be measured accurately, as they are ever-changeable themselves, varying with the amount of cold storage they have had, their growing region, their color, and, of course, their size. Onions can be sweet enough to eat raw (Vidalia onions are one Georgia version) or so sharp and bitter, they can make you cry. The aroma warms a cold house as they sauté in a pan, caramelizing for a rich onion soup or to top a steak. They can be so mild they can hardly be tasted, as in a homemade tomato sauce. There are two categories of onions: spring/summer fresh onions and fall/winter storage onions.

All fresh onions—red, yellow, and white—emerge from the ground in the spring and summer, March through August. Fresh onions have a thin layer of skin and are sweeter than onions that have been stored. Spring-summer onions are best for salads, sandwiches, and light spring and summer dishes. While some do not like caramelized spring and summer onions, I think they are the best because they are indeed sweeter.

After the spring and summer onions are past their moment, all varieties are stored, usually in cold storage in the South. Called fall-winter storage onions, these are available from August to March. As they dry out, they develop layers of thick, light brown, brittle skin. Their flavor is intense, their odor is sharper, and they are more likely to make the cook cry when chopping them. They keep their flavor when cooked for a long time.

When an onion is first picked, the outside is moist. I've seen onions pulled and laid on the ground or rack to dry, and then returned to find an outside layer of their skin dry. Each subsequent dry layer is an indication of an onion's age and treatment. They get wet and gummy inside if they age too long outdoors, and if not stored properly, will turn gray-black and rotten, their odor a far cry from enticing.

According to the onion council, the greatest percentage of harvested onions are yellow; they are the kitchen workers and are adaptable to almost anything. Red onions comprise only around 10 percent of those harvested; they add color to salads and sandwiches and grill very prettily. White onions are only 5 percent of the harvest; they are sweeter and are primarily used in specialty cuisines, such as Mexican.

STORING ONIONS

Store onions uncovered in a basket or other airy place, separated from potatoes and other vegetables, and avoid refrigeration.

PREPARING ONIONS

Some definitions are in order that apply to home cooking rather than the rigid definitions of a culinary school. It is important to know that every one of these will yield a different measure of onion to start, although once cooked and the water extruded, they will wind up roughly the same in volume but not in flavor or texture.

The macho manner the chefs use—Cutting off both ends of the onion and then proceeding is silly in that the greatest source of the enzyme that causes tearing of the eyes is in the root end of the onion. For this reason and to keep their mascara on, home cooks are especially encouraged to retain the root until the onion has been chopped or sliced.

The first step for either chopping or slicing:

Cut the onion in half from stem end to root, leaving the root intact. Peel the onion and discard the peel or save for stock or dying fabric or Easter eggs. Lay the flat side of both halves of the onion down, so the cut surface is not exposed and the flat surface enables a firm grasp.

Chopping—This method is preferred when small pieces are desired, perhaps for cooking, as in a soup, or when they are to be combined, as with tomatoes for a salsa. Chopped onions may be purchased frozen and are very handy in emergencies (which in Cynthia's house is sometimes the difference in putting a stew on the stove or not).

Holding the peeled and halved onion with the fingers of one hand, cut into the peeled onion half at regular intervals parallel to the work surface, working from the stem end to a quarter of an inch from the root. Holding the cut portions together with one hand, slice down perpendicular to the cut portions, keeping the slices parallel and roughly the same size. Stop when about $1/4$ inch from the root of the onion.

Dicing—Smaller than chopped, this method is preferred when absolutely uniform product is required. Dicing is used for garnishing as well as in the uses noted above for chopping. Other words instructions may note are "minced" or "very finely chopped" to describe a similar product. Dicing is rarely used in this book.

Slicing—Hold the peeled onion half with the fingers of one hand, knuckles toward the knife and fingers tucked under. Move the knife up and down on the peeled onion half, starting at the stem (not root) end and moving toward the root, in a steady back and forth motion, trying to maintain the same distance between slices. Stop a quarter of an inch or so from the root and save the remainder of the onion for stock or discard.

Sliced $1/2$ inch thick or more is preferred by some for fried onion rings and for raw onions on hamburgers.

Sliced $1/3$ to $1/2$ inch thick is the ideal size for caramelizing, cooking long and slowly until all the natural sugars come out. Also called "sliced roughly" these may take up to an hour to caramelize, but it is well worth it.

Sliced somewhere around $1/4$ inch thick, the onion is most often cooked over medium or low heat until it is translucent. Caramelizing is tricky but can be done if a low heat is used along with a great deal of patience.

Sliced about $1/8$ inch thick, the onions are transparent and are usually served raw, as on a hamburger, in a salad, or as a garnish. It is difficult to cook very thin onions, as they may burn quickly and lose all their juices, becoming dry and hard.

MEASURING ONIONS

Chop an onion the size and color most frequently purchased. Measure in a dry measuring cup. That equals one onion for the recipes used in your home. When larger onions are purchased, estimate accordingly. If recipes taste a little bland or less "oniony" than desired, up the amount considered as one onion.

COOKING ONIONS

Although an onion may certainly be cooked in the microwave, without fat in a nonstick frying pan, or in water until the water evaporates, these methods do not render the most flavor.

The preferred method is to heat a heavy frying pan. When very hot, add a teaspoon of butter or other fat such as oil or drippings. There should be a sizzling and a singing in the pan. A mixture of butter and vegetable oil will take a higher heat without burning than if butter alone is used, and vegetable oil alone takes an even higher heat.

Add 2 onions, sliced or chopped, depending on the need. After the great sizzling subsides, salt the onions as liberally as desired, reduce the heat, and continue cooking over low heat until some of the onions' water is extruded by the salt.

SHALLOTS

Depending on the variety, shallots have one or several bulbs. One shallot can be whatever amount the cook wants it to be. Measure a typical shallot and use that as a consistent amount. It can be blue-gray (French) or rusty colored (American), and the exterior varies.

Tasting like a cross between onion and garlic, shallots did not become widely available in the South until the late 1970s to early 1980s, although they were readily available in Europe. Some cooks substitute scallions for shallots, but I prefer combining a small amount of onion and garlic.

One chopped shallot is approximately 2 tablespoons, but recently we've found they can be double or triple that size.

Variations:

- Toss cut onions in the oil and, cut side down, move to a hot grill or under a broiler. Turn when lightly charred. May be made a day or two in advance and served cold.

- Top with herbed breadcrumbs, browned first in butter.

- Use 1½ pounds peeled whole shallots rather than onions, and reduce cooking time.

- Top cooked onions with goat or other soft cheese and oven-dried tomatoes and return to the oven for a few minutes.

TO SAVE A MARRIAGE

I've never heard of a man divorcing his wife because she didn't cook onions, but I've heard of plenty of marriages cooked onions saved. I once had a cooking student who attended only one cooking lesson, making it clear when she arrived that the only reason she was there was because her husband wanted her to be a good cook, and he had a fantasy of her staying home and cooking all day. She believed her hands were meant to hold charge cards, not a knife. When I ran into her several months after her solo class, I asked her why she had not returned. She looked at me, stunned. "Well," she said, "I learned everything I needed to know—I learned that if I cooked onions and garlic the second I hit the house, he thought I had been home cooking all day."

In fact, according to an onion source, men do eat more onions than women do. I've never measured my consumption of onions in poundage, but they have always been a necessity for my cooking. They would be my first choice for the "what would you take to a desert island" question. I decided this long ago when I found out they prevented scurvy and I wanted to be a pirate. Now it turns out they have many more antioxidant and medicinal uses.

CARAMELIZING ONIONS

Cook onions, stirring every few minutes, until the bottom of the pan becomes brown. If liquid from the onions gathers in the bottom of the pan, rather than browning, turn up the heat to remove the liquid, taking care not to burn the onions. Alternatively, heat another pan with some oil and butter, and move half the onions to the hot pan so there is not a deep layer of onions, which has a propensity towards "steaming" rather than caramelizing. When the bottom of the pan begins to brown, stir the onions so the brown goodness transfers to the onions. Continue cooking over low to moderate heat until caramel colored. There should be no excess liquid in the pan, but the onions should not be burned.

Hot water or stock may be added to remove the brown from the bottom of the pan, a process called "deglazing," which adds brown goodness to a gravy or soup. Sugar may be added at any time in the process, but a white onion in particular should not need any to be flavorful and rich.

Caramelized Onions

SERVES 6 TO 8

Caramelized onions are the basis for many dishes, and learning how to do them is important, as onions have a high water content and are somewhat reluctant to brown. Cooked too low, they will extrude water and never brown. Cooked too high, they will lose too much water and be crisp rather than tender. Divide between 2 pans to avoid overcrowding.

8 tablespoons butter or oil	**Salt**
6 medium onions, sliced	**Freshly ground black pepper**

Heat the butter or oil in a large skillet. Add the onions to the hot fat, reduce the heat, and cook slowly, adding a little salt, until the onions are soft and a golden caramel brown, about 30 to 45 minutes. Stir frequently. If the onions become watery, turn up the heat a bit, taking care not to burn them. Season to taste with salt and pepper.

Variations:

• Add a bit of sugar to the onions at the end of cooking.

• Add balsamic or flavored vinegar at the end of cooking, bring to the boil, and serve.

Caramelized onions are welcome in several ways:

• Spread over cooked green beans or inside a hot grilled cheese sandwich.

• As a condiment surrounding a roasted chicken, lamb, duck, or beef roast.

• For topping a pizza dough.

• By themselves, as a side vegetable, or accompanying liver or steak.

• Sprinkled with parsley or another herb, they can be a lively garnish.

Onion Jam

MAKES 1 QUART

This thick conserve is sweet enough to spread on bread but is a fabulous condiment on meats and vegetables. This technique calls for sweating the onions, covered, over low heat to extrude their juices before adding the other ingredients.

4 tablespoons unsalted butter

5 pounds yellow onions, thinly sliced

¾ cup granulated sugar

1 cup red wine vinegar

1 cup red wine

¼ cup dry sherry, optional

1½ teaspoons freshly ground black pepper

Melt the butter in a large heavy pot with a lid. Add the onions, cover, and cook over low heat for at least 30 minutes, taking care they do not burn. The onions will create their own juice.

Uncover and stir in the rest of the ingredients. Bring to the boil, quickly reduce heat, cover, and cook over a low heat at least 30 minutes, checking occasionally and stirring if necessary, until the mixture thickens like jam.

Cool and move to airtight containers, storing in the refrigerator up to 2 to 3 weeks, or freeze for later use.

STORING ONIONS

In recent years, the sweet Georgia Vidalia onion has been joined by Texas Sweets, Walla Wallas, and other onions developed for their sweetness and mild flavor. I particularly like them caramelized, as they are mellower than other onions.

Many Southerners purchase sweet Vidalia onions in 25-pound sacks. To feast on them all year round, keep the onions in a pair of clean pantyhose, knotting between each onion. The point is to keep the onions from rubbing together and potentially rotting at the point of contact. As the onions are bred smaller, they fit nicely into the toe.

Golden Vidalia Onion Tart
with Olives and Rosemary

Golden Vidalia Onion Tart with Olives and Rosemary

MAKES 1 (8- OR 9-INCH) TART

Vidalia onions are amazingly versatile—our Georgia Vidalias being among the world's sweetest onions—and they make for a satisfying tart. But any onion will do—even red ones. I also make this free form, just because it's faster and easier, and no special equipment, like a tart pan with removable bottom, is required. Try experimenting with shapes like rectangles and squares so guests don't just think it is an onion pizza but something extraordinarily special, which it is.

1 (8- or 9-inch) piecrust, homemade or store-bought

2–3 medium onions, preferably Vidalia, sliced 1/2 inch thick

Salt

2–3 tablespoons butter or oil

1 cup grated Gruyère, Cheddar, or soft goat cheese

1–2 sprigs fresh rosemary, leaves stripped and chopped

Freshly ground black pepper

1/2 cup Greek or other black olives

Prebake the piecrust in an 8- or 9-inch tart pan, and set aside to cool.

Meanwhile, prepare the onions. Heat the butter in a large heavy skillet and cook the onions slowly over low heat, stirring frequently, until they are caramelized and deep mahogany brown (page 130). This should take about 30 minutes.

Layer the onions and cheese into the tart crust, beginning with the onions and ending with a generous topping of the cheese. Sprinkle with rosemary and pepper. Lay the olives on a counter and swack them with the side of a large knife to loosen the pits. Remove the pits, slice or chop the olives as desired, and sprinkle them on top of the rosemary and cheese. Move to a rimmed baking sheet.

When ready to bake, preheat oven to 400 degrees. Bake 10 to 20 minutes, or until cheese is melted and the crust is a solid brown. Remove from oven. Serve hot or cold.

Variation: For a delicate layer of only onions and pastry, roll the dough into an 11-inch-long rectangle and bake it free form. Sprinkle onions only a couple of layers thick. Cut bite-size or larger.

PASTRY

Pastry always makes a splash at a party, particularly if it is crisp and flaky and the filling is a stand-out, with enough of a twist that it is clear it isn't from the grocer's freezer section. Although any tart can be made into mini-tarts or tartlets, a larger tart has the added advantage of giving substantial portions, particularly helpful for serve-in-the-living-room dinner parties with a small plate and fork. And it is much faster to whip up. Starter tarts—to be consumed quickly by those who have a drink in the other hand—are fine uses for grocery store pastry, particularly the name brand doughs sold rolled up in a box. Avoid frozen premade pie shells in a pan. A free-form tart is a better alternative.

PREBAKING A PIECRUST

Preheat oven to 375 degrees. Gently prick the bottom of the dough in the pie pan with a fork several times. This allows for the expansion of the dough. Crumple a 12-inch piece of parchment, waxed paper, or aluminum foil; reopen, smooth out, and spread in the bottom and sides of the pie shell, extending past the rim. Pour about 2 cups of raw rice, beans, or baking weights onto the paper, taking care to avoid spilling any of it onto the piecrust itself rather than the paper. Spread out on top of the paper to weigh down the bottom crust and push some of the rice or beans up the sides to stop the sides of the dough from sliding while baking. A roasting bag, as used for roasting chicken, is an ideal substitute for the paper. It can be filled with rice and beans or weights, put on the crust, removed, and reused at a later time. Move the pie pan to a rimmed pizza pan or rimmed baking sheet and bake on the middle rack of the preheated oven. Bake 15 minutes. (The paper will not stick when the crust is done but may if the crust is still raw.) When done, scoop out the rice or beans using a measuring cup, cool, and store them for use in another crust. Remove the paper carefully to avoid breaking of the crust. If this does happen, brush the crack lightly with water and press a small piece of the reserved layered dough over the crack.

Mix the egg and water together with a fork and brush over the bottom of the crust. Return the pie to the oven 6 to 8 minutes more to seal the crust. If the crust puffs up while baking, prick gently with a fork. Any holes or cracks can be patched with the reserved scraps of dough. If no scraps are available, dampen the area with a little water and push together as best as possible. Cover the edges of the dough with aluminum foil as needed to prevent over-browning when returning to the oven for final baking. If the filling is precooked or needs no further cooking, return the crust to the oven for another 5 to 10 minutes, until lightly brown on the bottom and a bit darker on the edges. If the filling needs further cooking, check regularly to be sure the crust is not browning too much. Reduce the oven temperature if needed.

SOGGY OR CRACKED PIECRUSTS

Sprinkling breadcrumbs into a prebaked crust helps keep it from becoming soggy. Another method is to brush mustard on the inside of the piecrust before filling and baking. If a piecrust cracks while prebaking, brush with beaten egg yolk, or sprinkle the bottom lightly with grated cheese before adding filling.

PEPPERS

Traditionally, red bell peppers were well-ripened green bell peppers. Now new varieties of bell pepper come in a vibrant array of colors—from white and yellow to deep purple—and are sweeter than green bell peppers, which have a harsher "raw" taste. A mix of peppers makes a stunning presentation.

Purchasing and storing bell peppers— Purchase bell peppers with smooth, unwrinkled skin and no soft spots. Store wrapped in plastic in the refrigerator for up to a week.

Once the peppers are roasted, they can be kept tightly wrapped for up to a week in the refrigerator. They will last several weeks longer covered with oil or vinegar, also refrigerated. They can also be frozen in plastic ziplock bags.

Although commercial jars or cans of roasted red peppers may be purchased in Italian specialty shops or gourmet food stores, hand-peeled peppers seem better. Try to avoid no-name canned brands. Drain before chopping.

BELL PEPPER VARIETIES

Bell peppers are bred and grown in many colors, a far cry from the green bells of my youth, which became red after remaining on the plant. The paler the color, the sweeter the pepper, with yellow and orange being the mildest, followed by red. Green peppers are the harshest, and I use them less and less. The seeds should be removed, but the peel is optional. I usually do not peel fresh peppers, although they may be peeled with a vegetable peeler.

SOME LIKE IT HOT

The size of a pepper is an indication of its spiciness. As a rule of thumb, the smaller the pepper, the hotter. Scotch bonnets are small and very hot peppers popular in Florida and the Islands, and one-fourth of one would be a very peppy ingredient.

SEEDING A HOT PEPPER

Wearing rubber gloves or small plastic bags on both hands, cut the pepper in half. Use the tip of a knife and fingers to remove and discard the seeds and membrane they're attached to. Store any remaining pepper for a later use or discard.

SLICING A RAW BELL PEPPER

Cut off the top of the pepper just below the "shoulder" to remove the entire stem end, exposing the ribs inside the pepper. Cut off the narrow bottom. Set the pepper on one end and make a vertical slice to open the cylinder.

Place the pepper skin side down on a flat surface and slide the knife along the inside of the pepper (with the blade parallel to the work surface), removing the ribs and seeds while unrolling the pepper so that it lies flat. Slice the pepper into strips, then into dice if needed.

Roasted or Charred Red Peppers

MAKES 2 CUPS

Whether served layered in a platter or cut into strips, there is nothing with flavor comparable to a red pepper.

4–6 whole or halved and seeded red bell or hot peppers

Preheat a broiler.

Move peppers to a foil-lined or nonstick rimmed baking sheet or broiling pan. Cook 3 inches from the heat until charred, turning so all sides are nearly black, about 30 minutes. Remove to a plastic bag. The heat and moisture generated from the bag aid in lifting the skin, making it easier to remove. Cool peppers sufficiently to handle. Peel off the skin with fingers; some prefer to do this under running water. Remove the stem, cut the pepper in half, and remove any seeds. Leave whole or tear into strips or chop.

Another way to char peppers is to push a large grilling fork into a pepper and hold over a flame, rotating it until the pepper is charred all over. This demands more of the cook's attention but is faster overall, although the stovetop has to be cleaned afterward.

Variation: Roasted Red Pepper Salad

Roast the red bell peppers as above and cut peppers into strips. Toss strips in a Basic Vinaigrette (page 196).

Variation: Roasted Red Pepper Purée

Purée roasted, peeled, and seeded red bell peppers in a food processor or chop until mushy. Press through a sieve to smooth completely. Serve as is, or add to mayonnaise, hollandaise, beurre blanc, or tomato or other sauces. A little Red Pepper Purée even enhances bean dips. Serve over asparagus, green beans, or your favorite green vegetable.

POTATOES

Not all potatoes are the same. They vary depending on the season, when they were harvested, how they were stored, and which of the thousands of varieties they are. The Russet potato, what we think of as the typical big Idaho potato, is the best for mashing due to its high starch content. A typical Russet (or Idaho) potato cooks up dry and fluffy, lapping up and holding the liquid without becoming runny.

Newer cookbooks tout the yellow varieties of potatoes, which have medium starch. Yukon Gold is the best known. Yellow Finn is growing in popularity. The yellow color indicates their richer flavor and that enables the cook to reduce the amount of liquid and fat added. The Yukon Gold is my favorite variety for mashing, even though the Idaho is technically better.

Old recipe books frequently refer to small red potatoes as new potatoes and have confused generations of cooks. The times I've been able to dig up and cook fresh potatoes are vivid in memory. Here's how to distinguish between different types of potatoes:

New potatoes—are newly dug and can be any size. They are sweeter than comparably sized ones that have been dug up sometime previous. The best of these are tiny—anywhere from the size of a fingertip to an inch in diameter.

Creamers—are the very small, early spring and fall potatoes that are newly dug.

Fingerlings—are a variety of small potato about the length of a finger. They come in many colors, from white to blue.

PURCHASING AND STORING

Purchase firm, earthy-smelling potatoes. Avoid any with soft spots. Potatoes turn green when exposed to sunlight, so store potatoes away from the light, but with ventilation. Do not refrigerate.

CLEANING POTATOES

Potatoes should be washed individually under running water before being cooked. Use a small brush or a specially designed scrubber as needed to remove any caked-on dirt, especially around the eyes. Small potatoes have delicate skins and should be treated accordingly. Large potatoes can be tough, and big eyes should be cut out with the tip of a knife or a pointed peeler. Resist soaking potatoes except to specifically remove the starch or to prevent discoloration after they have been cut.

PEELING POTATOES

Peeling raw potatoes—Peel the potatoes under running water and move to cold water to cover as they are peeled; keep cold—even refrigerated if necessary—until ready to cook, or they will turn brown (I usually peel just before cooking).

Peeling parboiled potatoes—Score around the middle of a potato. Cook in boiling water 15 minutes. Drain then immerse in ice water. They should peel easily and can be further cooked as decided.

TECHNIQUES FOR MASHED POTATOES

We don't know anyone who doesn't love mashed potatoes, and it's hard to make a batch that is a failure. But making them perfectly flavorful and fluffy is a technique that should be in every home cook's repertoire.

Besides the potatoes, the main ingredients are fat, liquid, and seasonings:

Fats—Use the best butter available, but goose and duck fat are delicious, as is cream cheese. An Italian chef I know uses olive oil and mascarpone, the cream cheese of Italy.

Liquids—In order to keep the starch in the potatoes from seizing and getting gluey, potatoes need to be prevented from cooling during the mashing process, so the liquid needs to be hot when it is added to the potatoes. Add some of the boiling water back in for family meals, but for special occasions try whole milk, half-and-half, buttermilk, or cream. Heavy cream will give a richer product. Skim milk will do a moderately successful job. "Hot" is the operative word.

Seasonings—The other common ingredients are salt and pepper. Although gourmets point out its harsh iodine-like taste, I use iodized salt unless specified. Use salt then taste after the initial mashing. Taste again before adding the hot liquid, adding more salt if necessary. Pepper should be freshly ground for so sacred an occasion. Freshly ground white pepper is ideal because it can't be seen in the finished product and won't sully the potatoes, but freshly ground black pepper is just fine. Just try to avoid stale old pepper shaken out of the box or can.

COOKING

There are two things to know about time. First of all, mashed potatoes can be cooked ahead of time and reheated. And next, how long to cook the potatoes varies according to their size and age. For that reason, they should be cooked ahead of time. It is simply too stressful to be waiting for the potatoes to be done when everything else is finished. And unnecessary. To speed up the cooking time, cut the potatoes smaller and cook in a large quantity of boiling water. If time is no problem, leave them larger.

Boiling is a misnomer. It is, as my teacher once said, "too violent" a term. Cover the potatoes in salted water, bring to the boil, reduce to a simmer, and cover the pot to speed up the process.

Testing—When the potatoes appear done, pull out one and cool it enough to hold a small piece, testing to see if done. Rub it between fingers. Does it feel smooth, or is there a tiny or larger lump? Take the potatoes off the heat and drain them if satisfactory. Otherwise cook them longer. Drain in a colander. Return to the pot over heat and let "dry" a few minutes. Once rid of the excess water, the potatoes will absorb more of the yummy stuff, and be lighter and fluffier.

WHAT KIND OF MASH OR WHIP IS DESIRED?

This is where memories of mother come in. If a mother had lumps in her mashed potatoes, they are craved; if she didn't, they may be abhorred—or vice versa. There are lumpy mashed potatoes that are delicious, smooth mashed potatoes that are satisfying, and even smashed mashed potatoes that are out of this world. Mashed potatoes can hold their shape stiffly enough to be piped on top of a shepherd's pie or so loose they run all over the plate (called "mousseline" potatoes). They can be mashed with a ricer, pushed through a fine sieve, or whipped (called whipped potatoes) with an electric hand mixer. So, the cook determines how lumpy and how runny they are.

Expectations contribute to happiness. If the texture doesn't suit, switch apparatus next time. But don't experiment at Thanksgiving when hosting guests. Save new methods of mashing for a family meal.

Mashing or whipping—A few minutes after "drying" the cooked potatoes, start to beat them with a potato masher or an electric hand mixer. A ricer also works. Insert the cooked potatoes in the ricer and press to extrude the potatoes. But avoid both a mouli-type sieve (one of those gadgets with a rotary handle over a disc with holes) and a wooden smasher, as both may result in gummy potatoes. Beat briefly, still over the low heat, until they start to fluff. If burning is a concern, add some butter to the pan at any time. Season to taste with salt. Add the hot liquid a little at a time and continue beating or whipping over the heat. Add butter, taste again, add salt and pepper, and the cook's work is done.

Keeping and reheating—Cover potatoes in the pan with some more hot milk or cream—about $1/3$ inch. Apply foil or plastic wrap to prevent a skin from forming. When ready to serve, remove the foil and reheat carefully in the pan over low heat, stirring in the liquid as it heats.

If cooking the potatoes a day in advance, cool and store in a well-sealed heavy-duty plastic bag. Move the potatoes to a bowl, cover with plastic wrap to keep a skin from forming, and reheat in the microwave until very hot. Or heat a pan with some butter, add the potatoes, and stir over heat continually until hot.

Freezing—I don't freeze my stellar, remember-me-forever potatoes, but I have frozen dishes that include mashed potatoes, like shepherd's pie.

Dried potatoes—One caveat: remember the rules. Use butter and cream, and don't tell anyone the truth.

PERFECT MASHED POTATOES

There are three crucial steps in achieving this ideal: 1) cooking the potatoes sufficiently, 2) adding fat to the hot potatoes to coat the starch molecules, and 3) adding hot liquid to the potatoes over heat to let the starches swell.

To check the doneness of the potatoes, remove a cube, cool enough to rub between two fingers, and see if lumps are gone. If not, cook the remaining ones longer. To finish the potatoes, select one of these methods:

• Mash or whip in the fat, then add the liquid over heat using a small electric hand mixer or sturdy whisk.

• Use a flat-bottomed masher or other heavy object to mash down the drained potatoes in the pan before stirring in hot liquid.

• Push the cooked potatoes through a ricer into the still-hot pan with melted butter.

Whipped, Mashed, or Riced Potatoes

SERVES 4

Certain meals demand mashed potatoes—certainly Thanksgiving is one. But to have perfect holiday potatoes, practice makes perfect. There are detailed instructions on page 140. Knowing the right pan, how much to make, and what family members like all take practice.

2 pounds Idaho or Yukon Gold potatoes, peeled and cut into 1/2-inch cubes	2 tablespoons butter
	1/2–1 cup milk, buttermilk, skim milk, or potato water, heated
Salt	Freshly ground black pepper

Add enough cold water to the potatoes to cover them by 1 inch in a heavy pot. Add 1 teaspoon salt and bring to the boil. Reduce the heat, cover, and simmer until soft, 20 to 30 minutes. Drain well in a colander, reserving water as needed to add to the mashed potatoes.

Add the butter to the empty pot and melt over low heat. Return the potatoes to the pot over a low heat and whip, mash, or rice as below to incorporate the butter. If the potatoes are more watery than desired, before adding the hot liquid, cook the potatoes with the butter until some of the liquid evaporates. Add some of the hot liquid and butter, and blend well. Continue adding milk, mashing or whipping constantly, until the desired consistency is reached. Season to taste with salt and pepper. If not serving immediately, cover with plastic wrap or foil and see reheating instructions on page 141, then whip, beat, or mash as described on page 140 and left.

Variations:

• Substitute heavy cream, cream cheese, or mascarpone for rich mashed potatoes.

• Leave peel on and smash potatoes in the pot with a heavy object.

• Add roasted garlic or chopped fresh herbs.

Roasted Potatoes, Onions, and Turnips

SERVES 6 TO 8

The earthy richness of large (baseball-sized) root vegetables makes them an attractive fall and winter dish. When I grew up, all the meat drippings were saved, usually in a metal can next to the stove. The drippings were mixed willy-nilly and no one was concerned. While drippings add an enormous amount of flavor and color, nut butter or oil works as well. This recipe technique calls for browning the vegetables first on top of the stove. Leftovers are good as is or in a salad.

3 turnips, peeled	4–8 tablespoons meat drippings, butter, or oil
3 medium potatoes, peeled	Salt
3 medium carrots, peeled	Freshly ground black pepper
3 medium onions, peeled	1 tablespoon chopped fresh rosemary

Preheat oven to 400 degrees.

Cut the vegetables into quarters. Cover the turnips with water in a saucepan, bring to the boil, and boil for 5 minutes to blanch.* Drain and dry on paper towels.

Meanwhile, heat the drippings in a large, heavy flameproof pan. Add enough of the potatoes to cover the bottom of the pan, brown on one side, and remove. Follow with the drained and dried turnips, also browning on one side. Cook the carrots briefly, browning lightly. It is not necessary to brown the onions, as they cook quickly; but if time is available, they will be a bit better if also browned on one side.

Return all the vegetables and juices to the pan and roast in the oven about 1 hour, turning every 15 minutes, until browned and crisp all over. Season to taste with salt and pepper. Crumble rosemary on top and serve hot.

Root vegetables become bitter when old or larger than a baseball, so they should be blanched (page 12). They add so much to the flavor of the dish that it is worth the effort.

Variations:

• Add quartered fennel bulb and cook as above.

• Green onions and shallot bulbs can be used as well.

Singular units, like baked potatoes, are hard to divide to serve more than one person without seeming stingy or skimpy. The same unit cut into small pieces will serve more people. It's like the loaves and fishes parable. Perhaps it is because there is less waste—each person eats only what he or she truly wants.

Ribboned Potatoes

SERVES 4

With the advent of new kitchen tools, there are many more methods of preparing and serving vegetables available to the home cook. The thinner a food is, the quicker it cooks. These ribboned potatoes are about as thin as one can get; once ribboned, they will cook quickly. Ribboned potatoes go further than baked ones, so this amount should be sufficient for four people. These are pretty on the plate, quick cooking, and light eating.

2–3 large potatoes, peeled	Salt
2 tablespoons butter	Freshly ground black pepper
2 tablespoons chopped fresh parsley	

To make ribbons, pare strips from the peeled potatoes with a vegetable peeler. Move strips to a bowl of cold water as peeled. Drain in a colander.

Heat the butter in a large skillet over medium-high heat. Add the potato ribbons and cook until tender, about 5 minutes, stirring constantly. Add the parsley, season to taste with salt and pepper, and serve hot.

Variation: Substitute sweet potatoes or try a vegetable mixture, such as potatoes and carrots.

Roasted Fingerling Potatoes

SERVES 4

Small potatoes are magical accompaniments to almost anything, from a vegetarian meal to hearty steaks and chops. Their crisp brown exterior and soft interior make them beautiful and scrumptious. They are a repeat dish in our homes, winter or summer.

1 pound small fingerling or creamer potatoes, well scrubbed and halved

1½ tablespoons oil

Salt

Freshly ground black pepper

Chopped fresh rosemary, optional

Preheat oven to 350 degrees. Oil a 15 x 10-inch rimmed baking sheet, or spray with nonstick spray.

Toss the potatoes with enough of the oil to coat; season liberally with salt and pepper. Spread the potatoes on the baking sheet, allowing room between them. Roast in the oven, tossing once or twice with some rosemary, until the potatoes are soft in the center and a rich brown on the outside, 30 to 45 minutes, depending on size. Sprinkle with more rosemary to serve.

Variations:

• Chop 4 garlic cloves and add to the oil before coating potatoes. Sprinkle generously with fresh rosemary before and after roasting.

• Cut Yukon Golds or other potatoes into 1½-inch chunks and proceed as above.

• Toss the hot potatoes in 1 tablespoon mustard seed and return to the oven for another 5 minutes. Remove and add 2 tablespoons Dijon mustard, tossing with a spoon to coat the potatoes lightly. Season to taste with salt and pepper.

MANDOLINES

Mandolines, ultra-sharp kitchen slicers, used to be relegated to professional kitchens. I've always been a bit afraid of their ability to slice off a finger in no time. Now there are many safer varieties available in cookware stores that offer more slicing options to the home cook.

OVEN-PROOFING HANDLES

Know the maximum temperature of your specific pans—check the directions. Most will take up to 450 degrees. Wrap any nonmetal handle in layers of aluminum foil. *Avoid using wooden-handled pans in the oven.*

Garlic-Flavored Giant Potato Cake

SERVES 6

One large potato cake is infinitely easier to cook than a number of smaller ones. It has an exterior crispness and brownness that far exceeds fried potatoes. Weighing down the potatoes in this recipe aids in pushing out the moisture from the potatoes, causing the potato cake to stick together as well as crisping the bottom of the cake. Potato cakes cut more easily with kitchen scissors or a pizza cutter than with a knife.

2 pounds Yukon Gold or other medium-to-large potatoes, peeled

3–4 garlic cloves, chopped

2 tablespoons finely chopped fresh parsley

1 tablespoon finely chopped fresh oregano

Salt

Freshly ground black pepper

4–5 tablespoons butter or oil

Preheat oven to 450 degrees.

Use a sharp knife, food processor, or mandoline to cut the potatoes into julienne strips similar in size to a long grate. Toss with the garlic, parsley, oregano, salt, and pepper.

Heat the butter until sizzling in a 9- or 10-inch heavy, nonstick or well-seasoned iron pan with a heatproof handle. Spread the potatoes over the bottom of the pan, then spread the rest on top. Cover with buttered aluminum foil. Press down the foil with the bottom of another pan or heavy weight. Cook over medium heat until the bottom is brown, about 10 minutes. Move to the oven and bake for 20 to 25 minutes, until the potatoes are tender and the bottom is crisp. Remove the foil and bake for an additional 5 minutes. Place a heatproof serving dish over the pan. Using oven mitts, carefully turn the cake out onto a serving dish.

Garlic-Flavored Giant Potato Cake

Oven-Crisp Potatoes

SERVES 4 TO 6

Thinly sliced potatoes brushed with oil and oven crisped rival most fried ones. Even better, there is no pot of oil to deal with or discard, and these can be reheated or even served at room temperature. Don't bother freezing this dish.

4 baking potatoes, peeled and sliced ⅛ inch thick

2 tablespoons oil

Salt

Freshly ground black pepper

Preheat oven to 400 degrees.

Slightly overlap the sliced potatoes in 2 large, well-oiled or nonstick cake or square pans. Brush with oil and sprinkle with salt and pepper. Bake 15 minutes, remove from oven, and flip potatoes to the other side. Return to oven and bake 15 more minutes, until lightly browned and crisp on both sides. Slide carefully onto a serving dish, gathering any stray potatoes back on top. Cut with scissors or a pizza cutter to serve.

Variations:

• Sprinkle with 3 tablespoons chopped fresh herbs before or after baking.

• Arrange 5 slices of potato in an overlapping flower design about 4 inches across. Top with 3 smaller slices. Repeat as necessary until all the potatoes are used and in a floral pattern. Brush with oil and continue with recipe as above.

Snacking Potatoes

SERVES 8

The friend who gave this recipe to me always kept a container of these potatoes in the refrigerator for her teenage children to snack on rather than chips or dips. These can do double duty at picnics or on the buffet table. If the creamers are very small, leave whole.

2½ pounds fingerling or creamer potatoes, peeled if desired, cut into 1½-inch cubes

½ cup chopped fresh parsley, chives, thyme, and/or basil

2 garlic cloves, chopped

¼ teaspoon Dijon or dry mustard

½ cup olive oil

¼ cup red wine vinegar

Salt

Freshly ground black pepper

Add the potatoes to a large pan of boiling water to cover. Return to the boil, cover, and reduce heat. Simmer 30 minutes, or until a fork comes out clean but they are not mushy. Drain well and move to a bowl. Whisk together the herbs, garlic, mustard, olive oil, and vinegar. Pour over the potatoes and toss gently. Season to taste with salt and pepper. Marinate at least 4 hours or up to a week, covered and refrigerated, preferably in a glass jar with a lid, stirring occasionally. Serve cold or at room temperature for a picnic, or reheat quickly in a frying pan or microwave for a buffet.

Simple Baked Potatoes

SERVES 6

There are times when a good baked potato is the best part of a day. Satisfying on its own, a favorite condiment can lift it to heavenly. If time is of the essence, insert a metal skewer through the potato before baking to speed up the baking time.

6 baking potatoes	Yogurt, optional
Salt	Soft goat cheese, optional,
Freshly ground black pepper	Mascarpone cheese, optional
Butter, optional	Cream cheese, optional
Sour cream, optional	Grated Cheddar cheese, optional
Chives, optional	

Preheat oven to 500 degrees.

Prick the clean, dry potatoes several times with a fork and move to a rimmed baking sheet or oven rack. Bake for 1 to 1^1/$_2$ hours, until done. Cut a vertical slit down the top of the potato to release the steam (which keeps the potato light and fluffy) and season to taste with plenty of salt and pepper. Although potatoes lose some quality when baked ahead a few hours, they still are satisfactory reheated at 350 degrees for 15 minutes. Wrapping in aluminum foil makes them soggy.

Serve with butter, salt and pepper, sour cream, chives, yogurt, soft goat cheese, mascarpone, cream cheese, or grated Cheddar, as desired.

Variations:

• If time is short, cook the potatoes according to individual microwave directions. Move to a 500-degree preheated oven and bake for 10 minutes to crisp the skin before serving.

• Hundreds of recipes for twice-baked potatoes exist. They call for scooping out the center of the potato, mashing it with cheese or other ingredients, and re-baking it. Create your own recipe and you can't go wrong.

Fingerling Potato Salad

SERVES 8

Since mayonnaise-based potato salads are frequently left out on buffet or picnic tables for several hours, when I take one to such an occasion, I use one made with a vinaigrette rather than homemade mayonnaise. I find the mayonnaise is not missed, and it is a relief to avoid anxiety about the salad making someone sick. (Store-bought mayonnaise has more acid, which is not dangerous when diluted by the potato and other juices, and produces a safe salad.)

Fingerling potatoes are a recently popular variety. Previously only large potatoes, usually Idaho, were the standard, making a mushier (if beloved) salad. For this reason, we give directions for cooking the fingerlings.

2–3 pounds fingerling, creamer, or small new potatoes, quartered if necessary	Salt
	Freshly ground black pepper
1/3 cup red or white wine vinegar	Granulated sugar
1 tablespoon Dijon mustard	Chopped fresh herbs, such as thyme or parsley, optional
3/4 cups olive oil	

Bring a large pot of salted water to the boil. Add the potatoes, reduce heat to a simmer, and cook for about 25 minutes, until fork tender. Take care the potatoes don't become mushy.

Whisk together the vinegar and mustard in a small bowl. While whisking, slowly drizzle in the olive oil and continue whisking until emulsified (page 193). Season to taste with salt, pepper, and sugar.

Toss the hot drained potatoes with enough dressing to coat lightly. Add herbs if desired.

Variation: Add crisp cooked bacon.

BOILING POTATOES

Small fresh potatoes should go into boiling water, just as green vegetables do. Larger, older potatoes, both peeled and unpeeled, usually quartered, can be substituted and should be started in cold water and brought to the boil.

Fingerling Potato Salad,
Snacking Potatoes, and
Old-Fashioned Potato Salad

Old-Fashioned Potato Salad

Serves 6 to 8

Store-bought mayonnaise with a touch of mustard was always the base dressing for potato salad in Cynthia's family (they swore by Duke's). The crunchy celery and onion are part of the satisfaction of this salad, but mince these if a finer texture is desired. Her grandmother always finished the top with a sprinkle of paprika.

2 pounds russet potatoes, peeled and cut into 1-inch cubes

1 cup mayonnaise

2 hard-boiled eggs, chopped

1/2 medium Vidalia onion, chopped

1 celery rib, chopped

1 teaspoon mustard seed

Salt and freshly ground black pepper

Paprika, optional

Bring potatoes to the boil in a large pot of salted water. Cook until just tender, about 25 minutes, depending on size of potatoes. Drain potatoes and move to a large bowl. Stir mayonnaise, eggs, onion, celery, and mustard seed together in a small bowl. Stir mixture into potatoes to coat them well. Season to taste with salt and pepper. Chill before serving. Sprinkle with a few dashes of paprika, if desired.

Robbinsville Fried Ramps and Potatoes

SERVES 4 TO 6

In his book Smokehouse Ham, Spoonbread, & Scuppernong Wine, *Joe Dabney writes that a sure sign of spring in the southern Appalachian Mountains is the deep green leaves of the ramp shooting up through the warming ground. A relative of the onion and garlic family, this wild leek is known for its pungent taste and aroma, which lingers like a cloud around the eater for hours. Celebrated with festivals in West Virginia, Tennessee, North Carolina, and Georgia, the ramp is used in small amounts as one would an onion in salads, or in larger quantities, as below, with potatoes and eggs as a meal-in-one. Look for them in local greenmarkets.*

1 quart ramps	3 tablespoons bacon drippings or oil
3 medium potatoes	3 large eggs

Wash the ramps, including the leaves, and cut into 1-inch pieces. Peel and chop the potatoes into 1-inch cubes. Heat the bacon fat in a heavy pan; cook the ramps and potatoes until the potatoes are brown and cooked through. Beat the eggs together lightly, pour over the potatoes, and stir. Cook for 2 minutes, until the eggs begin to set on the bottom; turn and fry on the other side for 2 to 3 minutes, until the eggs are cooked.

Pickled Ramps

1 cup rice wine vinegar	1 teaspoon coriander seed
1 cup water	1 teaspoon peppercorns
1 cup granulated sugar	1 pound ramps

Mix together vinegar, water, and sugar in a saucepan and bring to the boil. Stir occasionally until the sugar is dissolved. Remove from the heat and add coriander and peppercorns.

Clean the ramps and remove any greens where the green begins on the stalk for another use (excellent pan-sautéed to serve with meats or chicken). Cut off the root end of the ramp. Move the ramps to a pot of boiling salted water to blanch 1 minute. Transfer ramps to a bowl of ice water to stop the cooking.

When both the ramps and the vinegar mixture are cool, combine them in a 1-pint jar and refrigerate. Ramps will be ready to eat in about 5 days.

SUMMER SQUASH

Summer squash grow during the warm months and can seem to overtake a garden. They include pattypan, crookneck yellow, straight-neck, and zucchini. Small to medium-size squash are preferable to large ones. The larger squash tend to have more seeds and are more watery, and therefore have less flavor. Look for squash with firm, glossy skin. Store squash loosely wrapped in plastic in the refrigerator.

Every Southern gardener thrills to see the first zucchini of the season, and loathes picking it by the end of summer. As one of the South's most prolific home-garden crops, zucchini grows well in our soil and climate and has kept Southern cooks on their toes inventing new ways to bring the bounty to the table.

Similar to crookneck and yellow squash, zucchini can be substituted in most recipes calling for those squashes, although zucchini has a more distinctive taste. Salting (degorging, page 91) the sliced zucchini before using in casseroles intensifies the zucchini's flavor and causes it to shed about 20 percent of its water. Salting is a must to batter-fry or brown zucchini. Smaller zucchini contain less water, and needn't be salted, but by the end of the summer, the larger ones can't be avoided.

Summer squash, such as zucchini and yellow crookneck, are harvested and eaten while the vegetable is still in an immature state. Left to grow on the vine, they develop a tough outer skin, as does winter squash.

Sautéed Zucchini or Squash Blossoms

Sautéed Zucchini or Squash Blossoms

SERVES 4

Yellow squash and zucchini, like okra, have particularly tasty blossoms. The male flowers do not traditionally bear any "fruit," but they are mouthwatering stuffed and deep-fried in a batter (page 159) or used as a pretty, flavorful garnish. The female flowers can be distinguished by the tiny vegetable protruding from the base of the flower. The flower withers as the fruit grows.

2 tablespoons butter

1 teaspoon oil

1 pint (about 12) zucchini flower blossoms, lightly rinsed and dried

Salt

Freshly ground black pepper

1 tablespoon chopped fresh thyme or basil

Heat the butter and oil in a large skillet. When hot, add the squash flowers and cook, without browning, for just a few minutes, turning until they puff or burst into full blossoms. Season to taste with salt, pepper, and herbs. Serve immediately. The blossoms will deflate when removed from the heat.

Variation: Batter-Sautéed Zucchini or Squash Blossoms

Use the batter for Stuffed Zucchini blossoms, below, and fry as directed.

Stuffed Zucchini or Squash Blossoms

MAKES 12 BLOSSOMS

Stuffing squash blossoms with this recipe from my intern Chuck Lee and frying them in a light batter results in just a kiss of crispness in the blossoms, with a melting interior. This recipe can be increased as desired. Refrigerate the leftovers for the next day. Any extra stuffing can be refrigerated and used as a stuffing for grape or cherry tomatoes.

2 tablespoons oil

½ medium onion, finely chopped

1 garlic clove, finely chopped

1 cup goat or cream cheese or other soft variety, room temperature

2 tablespoons chopped Oven-Roasted Tomatoes (page 179)

12 squash blossoms

Fritter Batter (facing)

Shortening or vegetable oil for frying

Salt

Freshly ground black pepper

Heat the oil in a skillet until shimmering; add the onion and sauté 4 to 5 minutes. Add garlic and stir for another 30 seconds. Remove from heat and set aside.

Beat cheese with an electric hand mixer until smooth. Stir in the onion and garlic mixture and tomatoes until blended. Move mixture to a plastic ziplock bag. Cut off one corner to make a piping bag. Carefully open the squash blossoms and move the slit end of the bag into the blossom. Push from the top of the bag and pipe the mixture into the blossom to within ¼ to ½ inch from the opening. Gently twist the top of the blossom closed. Dip into batter.

Meanwhile, fill a heavy frying pan no more than half full of oil and heat to 350 degrees. Add the blossoms one by one and fry until light brown, reducing heat if they brown too quickly. Move to a paper towel to drain. Season to taste with salt and pepper. Serve hot.

Fritter Batter

MAKES 2¼ CUPS

Fine and thin, like the tempura batter used in Japanese cooking, this batter should be icy cold and made at the last minute. It is ideal for frying delicate goods such as squash blossoms or thinly sliced vegetables like squash and zucchini, mushrooms, green beans, and the like, as well as shrimp.

1 cup all-purpose flour	1¼ cups ice water
1 tablespoon cornstarch	Shortening or vegetable oil for frying
1 teaspoon baking soda	Sliced vegetables

Whisk flour, cornstarch, and baking soda together in a bowl. Add ice water and gently whisk together without overmixing. The batter will be thin and may have some lumps. Set aside until ready to use.

When ready to use, put a cooling rack on top of a rimmed baking sheet lined with paper towels. Pour oil into a large, deep pan to a depth of about 1½ inches, coming no more than halfway up the side of the pan. Heat the oil to 375 degrees, as indicated on a candy thermometer. Dip sliced vegetables into the batter and allow batter to drip until just a thin coating remains. Dip the edge of the vegetable into the hot oil and swirl in a circle for a second or two before allowing it to slide gently into the oil. The vegetable will sink at first and then float to the top. If needed, hold under the surface of the oil for a few seconds to brown. When cooked light to golden brown, remove with a slotted spoon to cooling rack and repeat with other vegetables. Serve warm.

Grated Zucchini

SERVES 6

Grated vegetables became fashionable in the 1980s. Until then, the idea of grating any vegetable except cabbage and potatoes was unknown. Interestingly, grating a vegetable changes both its texture and its flavor, a near-total personality transformation.

4–6 medium zucchini, grated

6 tablespoons butter, divided

2–3 tablespoons minced shallots, scallions, or onions

Salt and freshly ground black pepper

Move the grated zucchini to a colander placed over a bowl or sink and sprinkle liberally with salt. Let rest 15 minutes. Rinse, squeeze, and dry the zucchini with paper towels.

Melt 3 tablespoons butter in a large skillet. Add shallots and zucchini. Toss for 4 to 5 minutes over high heat, until tender but crunchy. Season to taste with salt and pepper. The zucchini may be prepared to this point several hours ahead of serving. Shortly before serving, toss it in the pan over high heat with the remaining 3 tablespoons butter. Transfer to a hot dish and serve immediately.

Variation: Mix equal amounts of grated carrots and zucchini and proceed as above.

Broiled or Grilled Zucchini and Red Pepper

SERVES 4

In only 30 or 40 years, these two vegetables have overtaken the use of yellow crookneck squash and green bell peppers on the grill and broiler. Even more water is extruded than usual when grilling zucchini, so the flavor is particularly intensified.

3 yellow or zucchini squash, cut lengthwise into $1/4$-inch slices

$1/2$ red bell pepper, cored, seeded, and cut lengthwise into 2-inch strips

$1/2$ tablespoon oil

$1/2$ tablespoon red wine vinegar

1 tablespoon freshly grated Parmesan cheese

Salt and freshly ground black pepper

Heat the broiler or grill. Brush sliced squash and red pepper with oil. Grill about 4 minutes per side. Remove to a large bowl and toss with vinegar and Parmesan. Season to taste with salt and pepper. Serve warm or at room temperature.

Layered Zucchini and Tomatoes

SERVES 2 TO 4

There's a natural affinity among vegetables that ripen in the same time period. The marriage of zucchini and tomatoes is one of the best. Degorge the zucchini (page 91), regardless of its size, to remove extra liquid.

2 small zucchini, trimmed and sliced lengthwise into 1/4-inch slices

1/2 teaspoon salt, plus more for degorging zucchini

2 tomatoes, cut horizontally into 1/4-inch slices and drained on paper towels

1/2 teaspoon freshly ground black pepper

1/2 cup breadcrumbs or panko

1/2 tablespoon chopped fresh oregano

1/2 cup grated Swiss cheese

1/2 cup freshly grated Parmesan cheese

1 1/2 tablespoons butter

Preheat oven to 400 degrees. Butter a 9 x 9-inch baking dish.

Sprinkle the sliced zucchini with salt and move to a colander placed over a bowl or sink. Let rest 15 minutes. Rinse and dry the zucchini.

Layer half the zucchini in the baking dish. Follow with half the tomatoes. Sprinkle with salt and pepper.

Mix together the breadcrumbs, oregano, and cheeses. Sprinkle half over the zucchini and tomatoes. Repeat layering one more time, ending with cheese mixture. Dot with butter and bake until golden brown and bubbly, 20 to 25 minutes. May be made several days ahead and reheated. Leftovers freeze fine for the family.

Stuffed Squash and Zucchini Boats

Stuffed Squash and Zucchini Boats

SERVES 6

No vegetables are consistent in size. It is better to have extra stuffing than not enough, and the extra can be refrigerated or frozen for another time or baked in a ramekin for a cook's treat. This recipe will also work for those canoe-sized, end-of-season zucchini; just be sure to cook them longer.

6 small zucchini or yellow squash, or a combination

6 tablespoons butter, divided

1 onion, chopped

2 garlic cloves, chopped

1 cup grated cheese, preferably Gruyère and fresh Parmesan

2–3 tablespoons chopped fresh herbs such as thyme, oregano, or basil, optional

Salt

Freshly ground black pepper

½ cup breadcrumbs or panko

Preheat oven to 350 degrees.

Halve the squash lengthwise and scoop out the pulp, leaving the inside walls of the vegetable intact to form boats; set aside. Chop any broken squash and add to the pulp as necessary to fill the other boats. Cook the boats in the microwave until soft, just a few minutes; or add to a pot of boiling water and cook until soft, approximately 10 minutes, and drain.

Meanwhile, melt 3 tablespoons butter in a heavy saucepan. Add the onion and any chopped squash, and cook until the onion is translucent. Add the garlic and cook 1 minute more. Cool slightly and add the cheese. Taste for seasoning, add the herbs, and season with salt and pepper.

Move the boats to a rimmed baking sheet and fill with the mixture. Top the boats with breadcrumbs and dot with remaining butter. Bake 15 minutes, or until heated through. Serve hot. May be refrigerated or frozen, wrapped well. Defrost and reheat until heated through, approximately 15 minutes.

Squash Casserole

SERVES 6 TO 8

Southern sideboards groan under the weight of luscious casseroles like this classic dish. This is without a doubt the most popular recipe I've ever included in a cookbook. The squash will taste better if sautéed first.

1¼ cups butter, divided

2 medium onions, chopped

1 green bell pepper, cored, seeded, and chopped

1 red bell pepper, cored, seeded, and chopped

2 garlic cloves, finely chopped

2 pounds yellow crookneck or zucchini squash, sliced

2 cups grated sharp Cheddar cheese or Gruyère, divided

4 large eggs, beaten to mix

1½ cups chopped pecans, divided

Hot sauce or Tabasco, optional

1 cup breadcrumbs or panko

Preheat oven to 350 degrees. Butter a large casserole dish and set aside.

Melt ¼ cup of the butter in a large skillet and sauté the onions and peppers until soft. Add the garlic and cook 1 minute, then set aside.

Bring to the boil a pot filled with enough water to cover the squash, and add the squash. Cook until tender, about 10 minutes. Drain and return squash to the pot. Mash the squash until thoroughly broken into small pieces. Add ½ cup butter, 1 cup cheese, eggs, onion mixture, and 1 cup pecans. Season to taste with hot sauce, and stir well to mix.

Move mixture into the prepared casserole dish. Combine the breadcrumbs with the remaining cheese and pecans. Spread evenly over squash mixture. Dot with remaining ½ cup butter and bake 45 to 60 minutes, until bubbly. Serve hot. This dish can be made ahead several days, covered and refrigerated, or frozen. Defrost before reheating.

Variation: Omit the peppers and hot sauce if a more subtle, richer casserole is desired.

WINTER SQUASH

Numerous varieties of winter squash are available in the South, including acorn, butternut, and spaghetti. Grown in the summer, winter squash take longer to mature and are harvested when the cooler fall weather begins. Select heavy, firm squash, as they will have moist, dense flesh. Store in a cool, dry place. If out on the counter on display, use within a week.

Many of the recipes for sweet potatoes can be adapted for both summer and winter squash.

ROASTING SQUASH

Both summer and winter squash take well to roasting, becoming fuller and richer in flavor. Roast whole or halved at 350 degrees. To roast whole, leaving skin on, prick a few times to prevent splitting, or slit as on page 150. Bake until fork tender. To roast halved, dot with butter, salt, and freshly chopped herbs. Or top with grated cheese and continue to roast until melted, 5 to 10 minutes. Serve with roasted pecans.

Sorghum or Sweet Molasses Acorn Squash

SERVES 4 TO 6

Thick sorghum-sweet molasses was prevalent as table syrup during World War II, but is seen less frequently today, although the plant itself is a leading food grain. Maple syrup is a good substitute. Do try to get 100-percent maple syrup and not corn syrup with maple flavoring, which is quite a different syrup.

2 acorn squash, seeded and cut into ³⁄₄-inch rings

¼ cup butter

¼ cup sorghum, molasses, or pure maple syrup

½ teaspoon freshly grated nutmeg

Preheat oven to 400 degrees.

Overlap the squash rings slightly in a large baking dish. Melt the butter in a small saucepan, add the syrup, and cook 1 minute, just until bubbly. Pour over the squash and sprinkle with nutmeg. Cover the pan with foil and bake for 30 minutes. Uncover and bake 10 minutes more, or until the squash is tender.

SWEET POTATOES

Sweet potatoes are available year-round and especially in the fall or winter after the first freeze. They are not botanically related to yams but are frequently called yams, particularly when canned, causing great confusion. Canned "yams" can be used like sweet potatoes. Sweet potatoes should be stored in a cool place but not refrigerated. They should be firm and uniformly shaped.

The skin is full of nutrients, so use it when possible. Scrub the skin with a soft brush under cold running water to remove any dirt.

Snacking Sweet Potatoes with Pecans

SERVES 4 TO 6

These are even better than sweet potato chips because of the caramelization around the edges. It is the first way I cook sweet potatoes when they come into season, anticipated for weeks. Don't be afraid of caramelizing them—most of us love the added flavor.

3 sweet potatoes

6–8 tablespoons butter, divided

½ cup chopped or halved pecans

Peel the sweet potatoes and slice as thinly as possible. (A mandoline will work to slice younger sweet potatoes but will frequently balk at older, tougher ones.) Heat 3 tablespoons butter in a large heavy skillet. Add enough potatoes to cover the bottom of the pan. Cook until lightly browned and puffy, with perhaps a speck of black in them. Turn gently and brown the other side. Remove to a serving dish. Continue in batches, adding more butter as needed and cooking until lightly browned. Add the remaining 2 tablespoons of butter to the skillet, toss in the pecans, and brown lightly. Pour over the potatoes. Serve hot, but these are delicious at any temperature.

Variation: Cut the potatoes into ½-inch slices and proceed as above, cooking the potatoes through.

Skillet-Cooked Brown Sugar Sweet Potatoes

SERVES 4

The famed Southern sweet tooth is bared for all to see when it comes to sweet potatoes and brown sugar. This is certainly a family or holiday favorite.

4 medium sweet potatoes	¹/₂ cup butter
Water	1 teaspoon salt
¹/₂–1 cup light or dark brown sugar	¹/₂–1 cup roasted chopped pecans

Peel the potatoes, cut them into 2-inch-thick slices, and move to a wide, heavy skillet. Add water to a quarter of the way up the sides of the pan, cover, and cook slowly until they can be pierced with a fork.

Remove from the heat and drain water from the pan. Sprinkle the sugar over the potatoes, add butter and salt, and return to low heat. Cook slowly, uncovered, until the liquid is sticky. Toss in pecans and serve hot. May be made in advance and reheated.

BOILING SWEET POTATOES

Boiling sweet potatoes is like boiling any other potato: cover peeled and cubed sweet potatoes with water and bring to the boil. Reduce heat, cover, and simmer until tender when pierced with a fork.

MASHED SWEET POTATOES

Baked or boiled sweet potatoes mash easily. If boiled, drain liquid and return sweet potatoes to the hot pot. Add ¹/₂ cup butter and ¹/₂ cup light or dark brown sugar. Mash with a fork or potato masher, or whip with an electric mixer. If baked, scoop the flesh from the sweet potatoes into a large bowl. Add butter and brown sugar, and mash or whip as above.

Sweet Potato and Turnip Gratin

Sweet Potato and Turnip Gratin

SERVES 10 TO 12

An exciting alternative to a potato gratin, turnips and sweet potatoes complement each other beautifully, particularly when large turnips are blanched to remove their bitterness.

2–3 pounds white turnips, peeled and cut into ¼-inch-thick slices

2–3 pounds sweet potatoes, peeled and cut into ¼-inch-thick slices

½ cup butter, divided

1–2 tablespoons finely chopped fresh thyme, oregano, or tarragon, divided

Salt

Freshly ground black pepper

1½ cups grated Parmesan and/or Gruyère cheese, divided

1 cup breadcrumbs or panko

2 cups heavy cream

Preheat oven to 350 degrees. Butter a 3-quart casserole dish.

To remove their bitterness, add turnips to a pot of boiling water, cook for 5 minutes to blanch them, and then drain thoroughly.

Gently combine the turnips and sweet potatoes. Cover the bottom of the casserole with half of the vegetables and dot with ¼ cup butter. Sprinkle generously with half of the herbs, salt, and pepper, and cover with half the cheese. Make another layer, finishing off with the herbs, butter, and cheese. Pour the cream around the sides. Cover with foil.

Bake until the vegetables are soft but not mushy, about 1 hour. Remove the foil, top with breadcrumbs, dot with remaining ¼ cup butter, and bake an additional 30 minutes. May be made several days ahead or frozen up to 3 months. Defrost in the refrigerator and reheat for 30 to 45 minutes in the oven, or reheat in the microwave, uncovered.

Variations:

• Use turnips and no sweet potatoes for Turnip Gratin.

• Use sweet potatoes and no turnips for Sweet Potato Gratin.

• Use a combination of zucchini and/or white potatoes.

Twice-Baked Stuffed Sweet Potatoes with Greens

SERVES 8

Greens and sweet potatoes arrive in the kitchen at around the same time in the fall as hog-killing time. In celebration of their compatibility, this dish dolls up the potatoes with bacon and greens.

4 medium sweet potatoes, unpeeled and washed

6 slices bacon, cooked crisp and crumbled, drippings reserved

4 green onions or scallions, sliced

1 cup cooked chopped greens, fresh or frozen, drained

¼ cup butter, softened

½ cup heavy cream, heated

½ cup freshly grated Parmesan cheese

Ground hot red pepper

Salt

Freshly ground black pepper

1 cup finely grated Gruyère or Swiss cheese

Preheat oven to 350 degrees.

Pierce the sweet potatoes with a knife several times. Bake 60 to 75 minutes, until soft. When cool, slice each potato in half lengthwise. Hollow out the center with a spoon, taking care to leave the skin intact. Move the flesh to a bowl.

Reheat 2 tablespoons of the reserved drippings in a heavy skillet. Add the green onions and sauté briefly over medium heat. Add the crumbled bacon and greens. Stir and set aside.

Whip the sweet potatoes with an electric hand mixer or mash them with a potato masher in a large bowl until smooth, adding the butter, cream, and Parmesan. Season to taste with hot red pepper, salt, and black pepper. Fold the bacon mixture into the potatoes. Divide the mixture evenly among the 8 potato shells, mounding the mixture; top with the Gruyère. The potatoes can be made ahead to this point. Bake the room-temperature potatoes on a rimmed baking sheet until the cheese is melted and the potatoes are heated through, about 20 to 30 minutes.

TOMATOES

Ripe tomatoes are ones that make a tomato sandwich taste like a tomato sandwich ought to taste. When ripe, they leave white bread slightly soggy with juice. They taste like summer, lush and fulsome. Who can forget their first ripe tomato of the season? Tomatoes can be beautiful or funny-looking—bifurcated, scalloped, black, nearly blue, deep red, yellow and red, striped red and green, oval, or fat and bumpy.

Tomatoes prefer not to be refrigerated and are best when allowed to sit a day or two after being picked.

There are over five thousand varieties of heirloom tomatoes. Their names are exotic, and some, like the Brandywine, are as generic as "Chablis" is to white wine, with many permutations. Although the name "heirloom tomatoes" was supposed to mean seeds that have been passed down and are not hybrids, the category is much vaguer than that, and not all heirlooms are heirlooms. Most recently, there are new versions coming in from Russia and the Eastern Bloc, for instance.

Slicing a tomato—Cut tomato in half lengthwise through the stem end. Turn cut side down. Slice in desired thickness either horizontally or vertically.

Chopping a tomato—Cut tomato in half lengthwise through the stem end. Turn cut side down. Cut into tomato horizontally, from blossom end to stem end, parallel with the board, going up to, but not through, the stem end. Cut down vertically as in slices above, also not going through stem end. Cut down vertically again, perpendicular to the previous cuts, creating cubes.

Seeding a tomato—This is a true nicety. Halve or quarter a tomato. Slip fingers or a small spoon under the "throat" and push seeds out into a strainer over a bowl, reserving juice if needed and discard seeds. You may remove the throat (core) altogether using a knife.

Storing a cut-up tomato—Chop up a half-used tomato, sprinkled with a little salt and vinegar, cover, and refrigerate. The tomato will marinate in its own juices and make a perfect accompaniment to a piece of mozzarella, a nice addition to a salad, or a delicious snack on its own. It will last a day or two longer this way.

Freezing tomatoes—When too many tomatoes present themselves and there's no time to cook them, move clean whole tomatoes to a rimmed baking sheet and freeze. When frozen, move them off the sheet into a freezer-type plastic bag. They will stay there quite happily until time to use. They will be easy to peel, and although not suitable to serve raw or in a salad, they are a welcome addition to a conserve (like a ketchup), spaghetti sauce, soup, or a cooked dish.

TOMATO SANDWICHES

We would be remiss if we didn't mention tomato sandwiches. Spread a piece of white loaf bread with mayonnaise or butter. Slice the ripest, juiciest tomato available and place on the bread. Top with another slice of bread spread with mayo or butter. To serve for a starter or special function, leave open-faced, removing crusts, and cut into triangles. Best peeled for a fancy occasion, but certainly not for a private sandwich.

Tomato Pilau (aka Red Rice)

SERVES 4

Here is another recipe from Two Hundred Years of Charleston Cooking, *which is a recipe of William Deas, Mrs. Rhett's butler, and is made the same way as the Okra Pilau (page 121) but without okra, and using salt pork.*

5 slices salt pork, diced	Salt
1 small onion, chopped	Freshly ground black pepper
2 cups canned tomatoes	1 cup rice
$^1\!/_2$–1 cup water or chicken stock or broth, divided	3 tablespoons butter

Rinse the salt pork, add to a skillet with the onion, and fry until brown. Add the tomatoes, cut them with scissors, and cook over low heat for 10 minutes. Add $^1\!/_2$ cup water or stock and season with salt and pepper to taste. Stir in the rice, cover tightly, and let the pilau cook slowly, about 12 minutes more, until all the liquid is absorbed, adding the remaining liquid if the rice does not seem cooked. Just before serving, stir in the butter.

Variation: Terry Thompson's Red Rice or Pilau

Terry Thompson was one of those students of mine who far exceeded me in skill. Living in Louisiana, she arrived at Rich's Cooking School with a bottle of Tabasco in her apron pocket and used it whenever I wasn't looking.

In Terry Thompson's book *Taste of the South,* the recipe calls for a chopped medium green bell pepper and 4 chopped green onions, along with poultry stock rather than water. She adds bay leaf, basil, black pepper, oregano, salt, and Tabasco, of course, along with the tomato, discarding the bay leaf before serving.

VARIATIONS ON PILAU

Pilau is pronounced as many ways as it is spelled. I've seen one spelling of *pileau,* many of *purloo,* and *pilaf.* It is featured in many historic cookbooks with several variations of ingredients: chicken seems primary, as do tomato and smoked pork, such as bacon or fatback. This Tomato Pilau is also called Red Rice, depending on the region, or is known as Mulatto Rice, which Damon Lee Fowler suggests is more for the color of the rice than a racial allusion.

Nana's Breaded Tomatoes

Nana's Breaded Tomatoes

Fond memories of this dish brought Cynthia in the kitchen to replicate her grandmother's recipe. Complete with baking it in the white cornflower Corningware dish, it passed muster according to her Grandfather. Spooning down through the buttery, crunchy biscuit crumbs on the top reveals the soft and tender breaded tomatoes below. It's a very rich dish, so serve accordingly.

3 cups torn or cut biscuits in ½-inch pieces, divided

2 teaspoons granulated sugar, divided

1 (14½-ounce) can diced tomatoes, divided

½ cup butter, melted

Preheat oven to 350 degrees.

Coat a 1-quart baking dish with oil or cooking spray. Line the bottom of the dish with 1 cup biscuit crumbs. Sprinkle with 1 teaspoon granulated sugar. Top with half the diced tomatoes. Repeat. Top with last 1 cup biscuit crumbs. Pour butter over crumbs. Bake 35 to 45 minutes, until the crumbs are lightly browned.

Roberta's Tomatoes and Cucumbers

SERVES 4 TO 6

Roberta O'Neill Salma and I worked together when we were young women, and we've kept our friendship alive. She is a painter and she makes simple ingredients look like art, her food tasting as good as it looks. Her husband shops for the fruit and vegetables and is very picky. Salt brings out the liquid in the tomatoes, making a mouthwatering tomato juice. Omit the vinegar if the tomatoes are ripe and juicy.

2 pounds ripe tomatoes, cut into $\frac{1}{2}$-inch cubes

1–2 teaspoons salt

Freshly ground black pepper

$\frac{1}{2}$ cup finely chopped fresh basil or parsley

Up to $\frac{1}{4}$ cup red wine vinegar, if needed

2 pounds cucumbers, cut into $\frac{1}{2}$-inch cubes

2 tablespoons chopped fresh basil or other fresh herb, optional

Sprinkle the tomatoes well with salt and pepper, and toss with the herbs. Cover and leave 1 hour or up to 2 days to extrude the juices. Taste and add vinegar if necessary.

Sprinkle the cucumbers with salt and let sit in a colander over the sink for 30 minutes. Rinse well and drain. Stir into the tomatoes. Add chopped herbs if using, stir, and pour into a serving bowl.

Variation: Add a few thin slices of red onion.

Oven-Roasted Tomatoes

MAKES ½ CUP

Oven-roasted tomatoes are the twenty-first-century replacement for the sun-dried tomatoes of the 1980s. Roasting takes advantage of tomatoes in season for future use and also fortifies the flavors when they are not at their peak by evaporating moisture from the tomatoes and concentrating their tomato essence. I also roast my tomatoes when they are almost too ripe and nearly over the hill, rather than tossing them out. Select mostly any kind of herbs. As the tomatoes caramelize, they may get a little black around the edges. To many tomato aficionados, like us, this can only make them better.

2 pounds tomatoes

Salt

2–3 tablespoons chopped basil, thyme, or oregano

3–4 tablespoons oil

Preheat oven to 450 degrees.

Slice large tomatoes into ¼-inch-thick slices, or in wedges if small. Line a rimmed baking sheet with foil or coat it with oil. Add the tomatoes in a single layer, not touching each other. Sprinkle with salt and herbs. Drizzle the tops of the tomatoes with the oil. Bake for 30 minutes to 1 hour, or until the liquid has evaporated and the tomatoes are curled around the edges. Cool tomatoes, move to a container, and top with 2 tablespoons of oil. Use as directed in a recipe or freeze for future use.

Variation: Slow-Roasted Tomatoes

Cook 4 to 5 hours at 275 degrees.

Variation: Charred Tomatoes

Heat a large frying pan until very hot, adding 1 tablespoon oil and 2 pints cherry or grape tomatoes. Sauté 2 to 3 minutes, until barely charred. Season to taste with salt and pepper.

Variation: Roasted Grape Tomatoes

Halve the tomatoes and move cut side down onto an oiled or foil-lined rimmed baking sheet. Bake at 400 degrees 30 minutes, and follow directions above, taking care to check often as these cook more quickly.

Fried Green Tomatoes

Fried Green Tomatoes

SERVES 4

There are many varieties of fried green tomatoes, with batter-fried being the most prominently presented due to the movie Fried Green Tomatoes. My friend Cynthia Hizer was the food stylist for the movie and has stories of the many she had to make during the course of filming. Alas, batter-fried frequently get soggy in no time.

For me, the tomatoes star, and their combination of firmness and sharpness are enhanced when lightly dipped into flour or cornmeal—or, in this case, both together. Crisp sautéed crumbs trap in the juiciness to let it explode in the mouth.

Since the tomatoes are not dipped in a wet batter before being dredged in the mixture of flour and cornmeal, the mixture will not adhere to the skin part of the tomato slice. This is not a problem, but it can be avoided by peeling the tomatoes prior to slicing.

2–3 green tomatoes, preferably peeled	Salt
1/3 cup all-purpose flour	Freshly ground black pepper
1/3 cup cornmeal	Shortening, butter, or oil for frying

Slice tomatoes into $1/2$-inch slices. Mix flour and cornmeal together on a piece of waxed paper. Season flour to taste with salt and pepper. Coat both sides of tomato slices in flour mixture, dusting to remove excess. Set aside.

Meanwhile, heat enough oil to coat the bottom of a frying pan or cast-iron skillet until it shimmers when a drop of water is added. Coat the tomatoes again before adding them to the hot oil, in batches as necessary. Cook until golden brown, flip, and cook until the second side is lightly browned. The second side will not be as beautiful as the first. Drain the cooked tomatoes on a paper towel while frying any remaining slices. Serve hot.

Nikki's Roasted Tomato and Zucchini Lattice Tart

MAKES 1 (8- OR 9-INCH) TART

To call this a "knock their eyes out" pie would be fair. It's stunning. My intern Nikki Moore developed this recipe one summer from some ideas we batted around as we stared at a near-empty refrigerator. It is remarkably easy. Don't feel constrained to do exactly as we did—make another design.

1 (8- or 9-inch) piecrust, homemade or store-bought

1 cup soft goat cheese, divided

8–10 slices Oven-Roasted Tomatoes (page 181)

1 medium zucchini

2 tablespoons oil

1–2 tablespoons chopped fresh herbs, such as thyme or basil, optional

Prebake the piecrust (page 134) in an 8- or 9-inch tart pan and set aside to cool. If using a tart pan with a removable bottom, surround the bottom of the pan with foil to prevent the filling from possibly leaking out while baking.

Preheat oven to 375 degrees.

Layer the prebaked crust with $1/2$ cup cheese. Add the tomato slices, spreading evenly over the cheese. Sprinkle the remaining $1/2$ cup cheese on top.

Meanwhile, slice the zucchini vertically into long strips with a vegetable peeler. Heat the oil in a small frying pan, add the zucchini, and wilt just a few minutes. Cool sufficiently to handle and form into a lattice on top of the cheese. Make a horizontal row of zucchini, leaving space between the rows. Weave the remaining zucchini under and over the horizontal row, leaving a space again so the tomatoes and cheese show through. Moved to a rimmed baking sheet.

Bake 10 to 15 minutes, or until cheese is melted. Add herbs if desired. Allow to rest 5 minutes before cutting.

Variations:

• If no tart pan is to be had, roll the pie dough into a large piece and cut, using a guide or freehand, into a circle or square. Move to an oiled or parchment-lined baking sheet. Partially prebake. Fill as above.

• Omit the zucchini and substitute $1^1/2$ cups grated or sliced mozzarella cheese for the goat cheese.

• Omit zucchini and substitute $1^1/4$ cups pimento cheese and spread evenly in piecrust. Top with tomatoes and chill. Bake 30 minutes, until puffy.

Nikki's Roasted Tomato and
Zucchini Lattice Tart

Tomato and Basil Salad

SERVES 4 TO 6

The shape of food influences its flavor. Wedges of medium or large tomatoes, or halved cherry tomatoes, not only add interest and beauty to a salad, but absorb the flavor of the dressing differently.

1 cup arugula or watercress

1 tablespoon red wine or sherry vinegar

½ teaspoon Dijon mustard

½ cup olive oil

Salt

Freshly ground black pepper

4–6 ripe tomatoes, cut into wedges, or 24 cherry tomatoes, halved

2–3 tablespoons chopped fresh basil

Wash and dry the greens, remove any tough stems, and arrange the leaves around the outside edge of a platter.

Whisk together the vinegar and mustard in a small bowl. While whisking, slowly drizzle in the olive oil and continue whisking until emulsified (page 193). Season to taste with salt and pepper.

Toss the tomatoes gently in the dressing. Remove the tomatoes with a slotted spoon and place in the center of the arugula, drizzling the remaining dressing over the arugula as needed. Sprinkle with the basil.

Variation: Crumble fresh mozzarella, soft goat cheese, or other cheese on top.

Gazpacho Salad

SERVES 4

This recipe shows us how long this kind of cooling combination has been used in the South. At a time when there was no way to chill a soup on a hot summer day, layering tomatoes and bread with cucumbers, salt, pepper and onion, then pouring some tomato juice over it along with mustard and oil, made a very cooling dish in itself, the salted tomatoes and cucumbers extracting juices that became soupy. Gazpacho salad, adapted here from The Virginia House-Wife, is the basis for what became a soup.

½–1 cup biscuit or bread pieces, torn or cut in 1-inch squares

4–5 tablespoons red wine vinegar

2 tablespoons finely chopped fresh parsley

1 tablespoon finely chopped fresh basil

2 large garlic cloves, chopped

⅓ cup olive oil

Salt

Freshly ground black pepper

3 ripe tomatoes, cut into wedges

1 small cucumber, peeled, if skins are waxed, and thinly sliced

1 red or yellow bell pepper, cored, seeded, and cut into strips (page 136)

2–4 green onions or scallions, chopped

Toss together the biscuit or bread pieces with vinegar, parsley, basil, garlic, and olive oil in a medium bowl; season to taste with salt and pepper. Add the tomatoes, cucumber, bell pepper, and green onion, and stir to coat.

Variations:

• Toss with 3 cups cooked small pasta.

• Toss with 1 cup cherry or grape tomato halves.

MAKING GASPACHA-SPANISH

"Put some soft biscuit or toasted bread in the bottom of a salad bowl, put in a layer of sliced tomatas with the skin taken off, and one of sliced cucumbers, sprinkled with pepper, salt, and chopped onion; do this until the bowl is full, stew some tomatas quite soft, strain the juice, mix in some mustard and oil, and pour over it; make it two hours before it is eaten."
—From *The Virginia House-Wife* (1824)

The Virginia House-Wife stresses skinning raw tomatoes. Make the judgment according to the toughness of the skin and the shape of the tomato.

Tomato and Watermelon Salad

Tomato and Watermelon Salad

SERVES 6 TO 8

One time I took this to a covered-dish supper, where it had a lot of competition with fabulous dishes, and it became an unexpected hit. As we talked about it, we wondered why it had taken so long for watermelon to be integrated with cheeses and other savory mixtures. Whatever the reason, we've been missing out on a refreshing salad. It is a typical New Southern dish—mixing old fruits in new ways.

3 cups tomatoes, preferably yellow or orange, cut into 1-inch cubes or wedged

3 cups watermelon, cut into 1-inch cubes

Salt

2 slices bacon, crisped and crumbled, optional

2 ounces soft goat cheese, or crumbled blue or feta cheese

Gently mix tomatoes and watermelon in a medium bowl and salt to taste. Plate individually or in a serving bowl, then sprinkle with bacon, if desired, and cheese.

This dish is best enjoyed the day it is prepared. No further salad dressing is needed, as the tomato and melon make a tantalizing dressing on their own.

Variations:

- If there is any left over, whir it all together, with or without the bacon, to make a refreshing soup. A little mint or lemon balm adds a refreshing note.

- Additional food companions for this salad, other than the bacon, would be tender cooked white fish broken into small pieces, or slivered chicken breast tossed together with the rest of the salad at the last minute.

PEELING TOMATOES

Some tomatoes can be peeled with a specialty tomato or other peeler. Tough-skinned tomatoes are more easily peeled by cutting a shallow X in the blossom end of the tomato. Dip into boiling water, roll, and remove with a slotted spoon to a bowl of ice water. The length of time in the boiling water—a few seconds or longer—depends on the toughness of the skin. The skin will peel back easily with fingers or a knife.

Refrigerator Green Tomato Relish

MAKES 10 CUPS

The sourness of tomatoes that come too early or late to ripen is a special treat for those of us who enjoy a bit of a pucker every once in a while. Serve with just about anything, particularly meats.

2 cups apple cider vinegar

1 cup granulated sugar

1¹/₂ teaspoons whole allspice berries

1¹/₂ teaspoons whole celery seeds

2 or 3 bay leaves

2 large red bell peppers, cored, seeded, and cut into strips

2 large Vidalia onions, sliced or chopped

5 pounds green tomatoes, cut into 6 wedges each

Bring all ingredients except tomatoes to the boil, stirring occasionally. Reduce heat and cook 15 minutes, stirring frequently, until mixture thickens.

Add tomatoes, bring to the boil, reduce heat, and cook 15 more minutes. Cool and move to airtight containers, storing in the refrigerator up to 2 to 3 weeks.

Tomato Sauce

MAKES 5 CUPS

This is my homemade tomato sauce. I use a neutral oil, such as peanut, and let the tomatoes shine. It's always a good idea to use the best canned tomatoes available. A little sugar takes out any tinny taste.

¼ cup oil

2 small onions, chopped

2 garlic cloves, chopped

2 (28-ounce) cans plum tomatoes with juice, seeded and chopped

¼ cup tomato paste

1 teaspoon–1 tablespoon each of chopped fresh oregano, basil, and thyme

1 tablespoon granulated sugar, optional

Salt

Freshly ground black pepper

Heat the oil in a heavy saucepan. Add onions and cook until soft. Add garlic and cook briefly. Stir in tomatoes, tomato paste, and herbs. Bring to the boil. Taste and add sugar if needed. Season to taste with salt and pepper. Reduce to a simmer and cook partially covered for 20 to 30 minutes, stirring occasionally.

If the sauce gets too thick, thin down with water or tomato juice. If too watery, simmer enough to reduce liquid. Purée using an immersion blender, food processor, or blender, or work through a sieve if a smooth sauce is desired. The sauce will keep in the refrigerator, covered, for several weeks or in the freezer for up to 3 months.

TOMATO GRAVY

Few older recipe books even printed recipes for tomato gravy, but it lives in the memories of those who grew up with warm spoonfuls on biscuits, rice, chicken, or chops.

Heat 2 to 3 tablespoons bacon fat in a frying pan. Add 1 cup chopped onion. Sauté 5 minutes over medium-high heat. Add 1 chopped garlic clove and stir 1 minute. Add 1 tablespoon flour and stir until the flour just begins to brown, 2 to 3 minutes. Stir in 1 cup chopped peeled and seeded fresh tomatoes (or canned). Season to taste with salt and freshly ground black pepper. Cook 5 minutes, stirring well. Add 1 cup half-and-half. Reduce heat to low, and stir frequently while simmering 5 more minutes. Serve immediately.

TURNIPS

Small spring turnips with the greens still attached are a delightful vegetable needing only minimal cooking. The larger "storage turnips" are best peeled and blanched (page 12) before continuing with a recipe. Spring turnips can be stored for a few days in the refrigerator, and storage turnips will last a few weeks.

Turnips and Red Peppers

SERVES 4

Turnips meld well with bell peppers and make a striking contrast that is particularly good with quail and turkey. This may be made ahead a day or so and reheated.

1 pound red bell peppers

1 pound small white turnips, peeled

3–6 tablespoons butter, divided

2 garlic cloves, finely chopped

Salt

Freshly ground black pepper

Core, seed, and slice the peppers. Cut the peeled turnips into quarters if the turnips are golf-ball size, or into eighths if the turnips are larger. (Smaller young turnips can skip the next step.) Add larger turnips to a pot of boiling water and cook a few minutes to blanch (page 12); drain.

Meanwhile, melt 3 tablespoons of butter in a frying pan, and add the peppers, young turnips or parboiled larger turnips, and the garlic. Cook over medium heat until the turnips are tender when pierced with a knife and peppers are still crunchy; add more butter if necessary. Season to taste with salt and pepper.

Variation: Turnips and Apples

Substitute any firm cooking apple for the peppers. Cut into wedges, leaving skin on for family, and proceed as above.

Turnips and Red Peppers

Turnips and Cream au Gratin

SERVES 10

This is one of those unforgettable dishes—make sure it goes into your permanent repertoire. If I don't serve this at Thanksgiving, I see dour faces. Casseroles like this one are easily adapted when more or less ingredients are available than called for. Eyeball the amounts available, and adjust the ratios accordingly.

3 pounds white turnips, peeled and sliced 1/8 inch thick

Salt

Freshly ground black pepper

2 tablespoons chopped fresh parsley, thyme and/or oregano

3 garlic cloves, finely chopped or crushed with salt

1 cup grated Gruyère cheese

1 cup freshly grated Parmesan cheese

1/3–1/2 cup butter

1 1/2–2 cups heavy cream

1/2 cup breadcrumbs or panko

Preheat oven to 400 degrees.

Bring a large pot of water to the boil, add the sliced turnips, and return to a slow boil. Simmer young and small turnips for 3 minutes and larger ones for 8 to 10 minutes to remove excess sharpness, but still leaving a bit of pep in them. Drain and pat dry with paper towels.

Butter a long casserole dish that will accommodate 3 layers of sliced turnips and the cheese—preferably no more than 3 inches deep. Spread a layer of parboiled turnips to cover the dish (they may overlap slightly) and sprinkle with salt and pepper. Mix the herbs with the garlic and sprinkle one-third over the turnips. Combine the 2 cheeses and sprinkle the turnips with one-third of the mixture. Dot with one-third of the butter.

Continue to layer until all the turnips are added to the dish, finishing with cheese on top of the third layer. Pour cream over the entire dish until it barely covers the top layer of turnips. Sprinkle with breadcrumbs and the remaining butter. May be made ahead to this point.

Add the dish to the preheated oven and reduce the heat to 375 degrees. Bake 45 minutes, or until the cheese is melted and the breadcrumbs are nicely browned. Serve hot. This freezes up to 3 months. Defrost and reheat in a 350-degree oven for about 30 minutes, or until bubbly.

VINAIGRETTES & SAUCES

EMULSIONS

Mayonnaise and vinaigrette dressings are made stable using a technique called emulsion. There are two main kinds of emulsions in cooking: 1) A temporary emulsion is formed by whisking vinegar and oil together with a bit of mustard or cream. 2) A stable emulsion ensues when two or more ingredients are held together by the existence of an emulsifier, such as egg yolk or cream, as in a mayonnaise and hollandaise. At this time the particles of fat are surrounded with the molecules of the emulsifier.

Acid is important in this equation as well, which is why prepared mustard (which contains an acid), lemon, vinegar, and other acids are frequently in from the get-go. There's always the pucker quotient, however, when no more acid can be added. This is where water helps. A simplistic mental picture I conjure up is that there must be sufficient air in the emulsifier for the oil to have a place to go. This makes it clear that there has to be a lot of whisking! All the ingredients, except the oil, are whisked until they are thick and light first, then about a fourth of the oil is added, drop by drop, until the mixture has thickened. Then the rest of the oil can be added in a steady stream.

Making a temporary emulsion from vinegar and oil usually requires beating about a fourth of the oil into the vinegar vigorously, drop by drop, as in a mayonnaise. I find it helps to whisk the vinegar and mustard together vigorously before adding the oil, just as whisking the egg, lemon, mustard, and water help in starting a mayonnaise.

A speedier process is to use a food processor or blender, adding the vinegar and mustard first and then slowly adding the oil. I find it bothersome to clean the appliance, but if someone else washes the dishes, why not?

CAUTIONS ABOUT HOMEMADE MAYONNAISE

It is important to keep homemade mayonnaise refrigerated and to use it within a short period of time, about 1 week; otherwise, discard it. Once diluted with the liquid from the potatoes, cabbage, or other common salad ingredients, homemade mayonnaise loses its low pH level and can be dangerous, particularly if left at room temperature. It is better to use a commercial mayonnaise in cases when you expect the salad to sit out for more than an hour or so, as its low commercial pH becomes a preservative to these foods rather than a detriment. The pH level of a homemade mayonnaise is too variable.

If mayonnaise breaks (curdles) or will not thicken, taste and add 1 more tablespoon lemon juice if it can use it. If not, add a tablespoon of water. This will give the oil a little more space and may thicken as well as repair a broken sauce. If not, whisk a fresh egg and a little water in a clean bowl. Slowly (drop by drop) whisk one-quarter of the curdled mixture into the egg. It should be thick enough to whisk in the rest in a steady stream.

Mayonnaise

MAKES 1½ CUPS

Mayonnaise is an emulsified sauce. It varies considerably with the type of oil used, so make sure the oil is one that will go well with the final product. Slaw, for instance, would be better with a neutral oil such as canola or other vegetable oil rather than olive oil—unless adding chopped peanuts, when peanut oil would suit better. For salads being toted to picnics and church suppers, a commercial mayonnaise is preferred.

3 egg yolks	Salt
3 tablespoons freshly squeezed lemon juice, divided	1½ cups oil
¼–½ teaspoon Dijon mustard	Freshly ground black pepper

Whisk the egg yolks with 1 tablespoon lemon juice, mustard, salt, and 1 tablespoon water until the egg yolks are thick and lemon-colored.

Gradually whisk in ½ cup oil, drop by drop at first, until the mixture becomes cohesive. Continue whisking, adding the remaining oil in a slow, steady stream, until the mixture is thick and the oil is incorporated.

Season to taste with the remaining lemon juice, salt, and pepper. If a lighter mayonnaise is needed, add 1 or 2 more tablespoons water. Keep covered and refrigerated no longer than a week.

Variation: Aioli Mayonnaise

We made this every day in the restaurant in Spain where I was chef. Add 4 crushed garlic cloves and ¼ teaspoon hot red pepper after the oil is incorporated.

Garlic and Red Pepper Mayonnaise

MAKES 2 CUPS

Made in a food processor, this mayonnaise is an incredible bump up from regular. It's a wonderful spread for toast to accompany a soup or can be used as a regular mayonnaise. It is even good stirred into some soups.

1 slice white bread

1/4 cup freshly squeezed lemon juice

3 egg yolks

1 tablespoon water

1/2 head garlic, about 5 cloves, peeled and crushed

3/4 cup olive oil

1 1/2 roasted red bell peppers (page 137)

1/4 teaspoon ground hot red pepper

Pinch of saffron

Salt

Freshly ground black pepper

Sprinkle the bread with lemon juice in a small bowl. Let sit until the bread absorbs the juice.

Process the egg yolks and water in the bowl of a food processor fitted with a metal blade until thick and lemon colored. Pulse in the moistened bread and garlic. With the processor running, add $^1/_4$ cup olive oil, drop by drop, until the mixture thickens. Add the remaining oil in a slow, steady stream. When it reaches the desired consistency, add the bell peppers and hot red pepper. Process until smooth. Add saffron, and season to taste with salt and pepper.

Variations:

• Add chopped chives or other herbs.

• Omit bread for a thinner mayonnaise.

• Use clam juice or fish stock instead of lemon juice to make this like the French sauce *rouille*, which is added to fish stews.

Basic Vinaigrette

MAKES 1⅓ CUPS

I keep this vinaigrette on hand in a jar on the counter, as we have salads nearly every night, and we use it up quickly. Give it a few shakes or whisk it when needed. It can be varied on a whim, adding herbs, spices, or whatever else suits my fancy that day. I use extra virgin olive oil most days. Always dress a salad at the last minute, preferably at the table.

Olive oils vary considerably, and some may be heavier than desired. If that is the case, dilute with a bit of canola or other light oil, such as grape seed. Salt and sugar take up the oily taste in a salad dressing, as does a bit of water or chicken stock. Avoid adding more vinegar than the recipe calls for, as it will just make everyone cough and still not accomplish the goal.

1–2 teaspoons Dijon mustard

⅓ cup red wine, sherry, Champagne, or other wine vinegar

1 teaspoon water

Salt

Freshly ground black pepper

1 cup olive oil

Granulated sugar, optional

Water or chicken stock or broth

For an everyday vinaigrette, whisk or shake together mustard, vinegar, water, salt and pepper to taste, and oil. Taste and add more seasoning, sugar, and/or water or chicken stock as desired. Refrigerate up to 1 week; whisk or shake as needed.

For a temporary emulsion, whisk the mustard, vinegar, water, salt, and pepper together in a small bowl. Slowly whisk in ¼ cup oil until thick. Add the rest in a steady stream while whisking. Season to taste with additional salt. Add sugar and/or water or chicken stock if still too oily tasting. This vinaigrette will be opaque and creamy, with the ingredients evenly distributed. Store covered in the refrigerator. If no stock is used, it can be stored on the on the counter.

Variations:

• For a small portion of vinaigrette, whisk together 1 teaspoon mustard, 1 tablespoon vinegar, salt and pepper to taste, and 3 tablespoons oil. Taste for seasoning and add sugar, water, or chicken stock, if needed.

• Use heavy cream rather than oil for a creamy vinaigrette.

• Add 1 chopped garlic clove; a chopped shallot or green onion; a favorite chopped herb (such as thyme, oregano, [ba]sil); a bit of curry powder, ground coriander, or cumin; or substitute honey for the sugar.

Vibrant Vinaigrette

MAKES ¾ CUP

2 tablespoons freshly squeezed orange juice

Grated rind of 1 navel orange, no white attached

½ roasted red bell pepper, torn into pieces (page 137)

2 green onions, or scallions, whites only, sliced

1 garlic clove, chopped

2 tablespoons Dijon mustard

2 tablespoons red wine vinegar

½ cup oil

Salt

Freshly ground black pepper

Granulated sugar, optional

Purée the orange juice, rind, red pepper, green onion, garlic, mustard, and vinegar in a blender or food processor until smooth. Add the oil in a thin, steady stream until the dressing is thick and emulsified (page 193). Season to taste with salt, pepper, and a pinch of sugar.

Browned Butter Sauce

MAKES ½ CUP

Browned butter has a rich, full toasted-nut flavor.

4–6 tablespoons butter

Add butter to a clean pan and heat over medium heat, swirling the pan until the butter foams and turns a golden brown, giving off an aroma like browning pecans. Pour over fish or vegetables.

Variation: Add 2 tablespoons lemon juice for fish or chicken, but not for green vegetables, as the acid will turn the green vegetables gray.

White Butter Sauce

A white butter sauce (beurre blanc in French) is a versatile and sophisticated sauce, served with vegetables, seafood, eggs, poultry, or meat. It's also a very good substitute for hollandaise and béarnaise, both of which require eggs. This sauce became popular in the South in the early 1970s. Even a failed white butter sauce will taste scrumptious stirred into vegetables, rice, or grains. Although it has no eggs, it is still an emulsified sauce. The main thing to remember when making this sauce is to be careful not to overheat it. While heat is needed to melt the cold butter, too much heat—as in rapidly boiling water—may cause the sauce to break, or separate into oil and liquid. A little practice will make perfect—finding the right pan and heat may take a few tries. Restaurant cooks use the apron of their stovetops, which maintains an even heat, to keep white sauce warm. Even if the sauce breaks, it is usable and may even be "saved" according to the directions below. If a sauce breaks, call it a melted butter.

²/₃ cup freshly squeezed lemon juice (or other acid, see variation below)

2 tablespoons minced shallots

1½ cups butter, cut into 1-inch pieces

Salt and freshly ground black pepper

Combine lemon juice and shallots in a small to medium-size saucepan. Bring to the boil and boil until the liquid is reduced to 2 tablespoons. If it is less than that, add water. Turn heat to low and whisk in the butter one piece at a time. If what looks like oil appears in the otherwise creamy yellow sauce, remove the pot from the heat and set it over ice, or add a little water or crushed ice to the sauce. Cooling it just a little might save the sauce from breaking. Season to taste with salt and pepper.

If the sauce is too tart, add a little water, more butter, or granulated sugar to correct. Serve right away, or cover the top with plastic wrap to prevent a skin from forming, and leave at room temperature or refrigerate. Many times, the temperature of the food will be sufficient to reheat it. To reheat the sauce on the stove, add a little of the cold sauce to a small saucepan over low heat. Whisk sauce until it thickens, adding additional small portions of cold sauce to the pan, whisking continuously, until the entire sauce is reheated.

Variations:

- A spoonful or so of Tomato Conserve (page 33) added to the completed sauce provides sweetness and color.
- Red butter sauce is made with red wine. Other acids may be used in place of the lemon juice. Try using ¹/₂ cup dry white wine or 2 tablespoons white wine vinegar, or a combination.
- Add 1 to 3 chopped garlic cloves with the shallots.
- Add 1 tablespoon grated or chopped fresh ginger to the lemon juice and vinegar.

ROASTING VEGETABLES

Oven-roasting vegetables allows the natural sugars to caramelize, giving a whole new taste dimension to most any vegetable. For all the vegetables here, line a rimmed baking sheet with foil, toss 1 to 1½ pounds of the prepared vegetable in oil, and spread out in an even layer on the baking sheet. Halfway through the roasting time, toss or turn the vegetables for even cooking.

Multiple vegetables can be roasted at one time. Cook vegetables of similar thickness and density together. Take care with timing and remove vegetables that cook more quickly as soon as they are done. Most vegetables can be grilled as well as roasted.

VEGETABLE	PREPARATION	ROAST
Artichokes, Jerusalem	Scrub, then halve or quarter	450 degrees, 18 minutes
Asparagus	Peel if desired, then cut off tough ends	450 degrees, 7–10 minutes
Beets, without greens	Wrap in foil	400 degrees, 50–60 minutes
Broccoli	Cut into large florets, chop stems into 1-inch pieces (see also cauliflower)	450 degrees, 7–9 minutes
Brussels Sprouts	Halve lengthwise, place cut side down	450 degrees, 15–18 minutes
Cabbage	Cut into 1-inch slices	400 degrees, 40–45 minutes
Carrots	Cut into 1-inch pieces	400 degrees, 20–25 minutes
Cauliflower	Cut into steaks	400 degrees, 15–20 minutes
Greens, such as Kale and others	Tear into bite-sized pieces	400 degrees, 10–20 minutes
Green Beans	Tip, tail, and string	425 degrees, 10–15 minutes
Okra	Slice into 1-inch pieces or leave whole	350 degrees, 9–12 minutes
Onions	Halve or quarter	400 degrees, 50–60 minutes
Peppers	Halve and seed	Broil 30 minutes
Potatoes, fingerling or other small potato	Whole, or halve if large	400 degrees, 45–60 minutes
Summer Squash, yellow or zucchini squash	Cut into 1½-inch pieces	400 degrees, 25–30 minutes
Winter Squash	Cut into 1-inch rounds or cubes	400 degrees, 30–35 minutes
Sweet Potatoes	Slice or cut into 1-inch cubes	375 degrees, 30–40 minutes
Tomatoes, fast	Slice into ¼-inch rounds or wedges	450 degrees, 30–60 minutes
Tomatoes, slow	Slice into ¼-inch rounds or wedges	275 degrees, 4–5 hours
Tomatoes, Grape	Halve, place cut side down	275 degrees, 3–4 hours
Turnips	Cut into wedges	400 degrees, 20 minutes

INDEX

Metric Conversion Chart

Volume Measurements		Weight Measurements		Temperature Conversion	
U.S.	Metric	U.S.	Metric	Fahrenheit	Celsius
1 teaspoon	5 ml	½ ounce	15 g	250	120
1 tablespoon	15 ml	1 ounce	30 g	300	150
¼ cup	60 ml	3 ounces	90 g	325	160
⅓ cup	75 ml	4 ounces	115 g	350	180
½ cup	125 ml	8 ounces	225 g	375	190
⅔ cup	150 ml	12 ounces	350 g	400	200
¾ cup	175 ml	1 pound	450 g	425	220
1 cup	250 ml	2¼ pounds	1 kg	450	230

With the ever-growing variety of vegetables and ways to cook them, it is no wonder that the largest, and coincidentally our favorite, chapter in our book *Mastering the Art of Southern Cooking* is "Vegetables and Sides." Here, in our new book, we present our favorite vegetable recipes from that book alongside many new ones. We have tried to enhance the flavors for which Southern cooking is known with new techniques and ingredients while also retaining the traditional. There's something delicious here for everyone.

Nathalie Dupree is the author of 15 previous cookbooks, having sold over half a million copies. She has hosted more than 300 national and international cooking shows, which have aired since 1986 on PBS, the Food Network, and the Learning Channel. She has appeared many times on the *Today Show* and *Good Morning America*. Nathalie has won wide recognition for her work, including three James Beard Awards and numerous others. She is best known for her approachability and her understanding of Southern cooking, having started the New Southern Cooking movement that is now found in many restaurants throughout the United States. She has been chef in three restaurants—in Majorca, Spain, Georgia and Virginia. For 10 years she directed Rich's Cooking School in Atlanta, where she stopped counting at 10,000 students. She was awarded the honor of "Grande Dame" for Les Dames d'Escoffier. She considers it her highest honor, as it is from women who have excelled in the food industry. She was also named the 2013 Woman of the Year from the French Master Chefs of America. To contact her, go to *Nathaliedupree.com*.

Cynthia Graubart, James Beard Award winner and *Southern Living* magazine columnist, is passionate about bringing families together at the table. Her previous book is *Slow Cooker Double Dinners for Two: Cook Once, Eat Twice*. She is the co-author of *Mastering the Art of Southern Cooking* (2013 James Beard Award) and *Southern Biscuits,* both with Nathalie Dupree. Her first book was *The One-Armed Cook: Quick and Easy Recipes, Smart Meal Plans, and Savvy Advice for New (and Not-So-New) Moms*. She travels the country as a speaker and cooking teacher, is a member of the International Association of Culinary Professionals (IACP) and Les Dames d'Escoffier (LDEI) and has served on the board of the Atlanta Community Food Bank. She and her husband live in Atlanta, Georgia. Join Cynthia online at *cynthiagraubart.com*.

Pepper

Cucumber

tomato

Eggplant

leek

Artichoke

Fennel

Chili

Champignon

Beet

Radish

Onion

Carrot

Potato

Broccoli

Avocado

Corn

Garlic

Pumpkin

Ginger

Pepper

Cucumber

tomato

Eggplant

leek

Artichoke

Fennel

Chili

bage

Beet

Champignon

Radish

Onion

Asparagus

Carrot

Broccoli

Potato

Avocado

Corn

Garlic

Ginger

Pumpkin